GUANTANAMO

Carlos Potes

Guantánamo

A Dysfunctional Romance

Carlos Potes

Kravitz and Sons LLC
1301 Farmville Blvd, Suite 104
Greenville, NC 27834

Copyright © 2011 by Carlos Potes
Second print edition (2025) by Kravitz & Sons LLC

| ISBN: | 979-8-89639-255-2 | (sc) |
| ISBN: | 979-8-89639-256-9 | (e) |

GUANTANAMO

Dan Durán is clueless, and Silvia, his cunning bride, knows it all too well. As a seasoned, trained linguist, he is artful in the interpretation of meaning; as a woman, she outwits him at every turn, keeping him in a state of permanent perplexity. The one thing they have in common is a completely different thing in each one's mind: a common means to different ends. An endless succession of mind games ensues as Daniel and Silvia pursue divergent goals that neither one of them fully understands. Charged with erotic tension and sardonic wit, the story unfolds in sunny Caribbean beaches and shady dance halls up and down the Americas, to the driving rhythm and taut, dynamic prose that make Mr. Potes's novella of dysfunctional romance a relentlessly compelling read. A thoroughly bicultural, offbeat tale of star-crossed lovers, Guantánamo is also a unique portrait of its time, with thought-provoking insight into the mystery that is America.

"Anything may be, and surely must, if you say so."

Sancho Panza

Cartagena

It rained all night, but for brief respites between torrential downpours, as if the bottom had fallen out of a great big bucket in the sky. Dinner had been unremarkable, at a landmark restaurant in the historic district of Cartagena, where the hotel shuttled us as part of a package deal Silvia had booked since before I arrived in Bogotá. At the time she told me it cost two million pesos, which I reimbursed her, but years later I found out it had been quite a bit more, and she had paid the difference. She had her reasons for keeping that secret, and others.

The shabby service we received compared to patrons paying full price didn't bother me, nor that the discount menu arranged by the hotel had none of the restaurant's better offerings. I was there for Silvia, and our first evening out in legendary Cartagena—that I'd always wanted to see but hadn't ever had a chance to—carried enough meaning to make it a memorable event whatever else happened. In the back of my mind I thought the trip was unnecessary, but she had insisted, and what self-respecting marriage should go without a honeymoon?

Passing up the shuttle ride back to the hotel, we ventured into the flooded streets seeking romance and adventure. Earlier I'd noticed an alley lined with nightclubs and bars, and thought we could have a few drinks, maybe dance a bit. A passion for dancing, for reveling in the movement of our bodies to the beat of the Caribbean music we both loved, was a bonding factor and a kind of foreplay that reinforced the physical intimacy we both acknowledged as a driving force in the relationship. Admitting it was just the honest thing to do: it was the simple truth.

We made it to the entertainment strip, not without first straying into a neighborhood that a Good Samaritan warned us to leave quickly, preferably by taxicab, if we valued our safety. Indeed, as we finally flagged one down, tire-deep in the overflow from inadequate sea-level drainage, a group of three men was already emerging from the shadows, ambling vaguely in our direction. Our benefactor had just narrowly averted our becoming a statistic in the city's crime files. We asked the driver to take us to a different kind of nightlife.

The clubs weren't very busy, because of the rain, plus May being low season in

Cartagena. We checked several of them out and finally settled on one that, although it was completely empty, played Cuban *son* and classic salsa that appealed to our lust for rhythm. We took a table under a large outdoor canopy, inches away from the rain falling all around us, that sprinkled us gently as it bounced off the sidewalk and sprayed on our faces as a fine, cool mist when the breeze blew through from the sea. The name of the place was Guantánamo.

We danced, drank rum and smoked cigarettes, which the owner, the waiter and the bartender took turns bringing to our table and lighting for us. The only other patrons all night were a few boisterous revelers that showed up in a bus as part of a nightspot tour, including a couple of drunk Americans that danced like bears. Their Colombian friends, showing them around town, were hugely amused at their cluelessness. We weren't. Soon they left and our crew of three resumed their pampering. They had adopted us for the evening.

Some cosmic force drove an ineffable magic, and we hung on each other's every word, though merely prattling, really, for the conversation was but a subterfuge, a soundtrack to the glances with which I told her that I'd never been happier in my life, and those with which she told me that she knew. At times the staff would join us at the table for talk—they'd tell us about their lives, their dreams, their family matters, hopes and disappointments. It was as if an ionized plasma field bound us all together in a moment of timeless transcendence.

How we danced! The music bore us beyond the realm of gravity, our bodies' synchronicity a mere reflection of the harmony of our souls, our hearts... wherever it is that feelings come from. We went home, to our transient love nest overlooking the Caribbean, waves crashing against the breakers ten stories below, and lay like children, searching through our naked bodies as if we'd just discovered them, her eagerness insatiable, my excitement never waning. How I loved her as the sun came up and I saw her sleeping body cupped in mine.

We had a late poolside breakfast of tropical fruit and coffee, followed by a cigarette and a stiff rum cocktail, which were dispensed freely all day long as part of the all-inclusive plan. The beach by the hotel was gray and unwholesome, and a large black woman insisted on giving me an "aloe" rub. Even as I declined it she proceeded to apply a goopy substance that she smothered on my legs and charged me 20,000 pesos for. Silvia was not amused but she really put her foot down when I was about to pay 50,000 pesos for a box of "genuine" Espléndidos.

If I did that, she said, she'd go back to the room, pack up and leave. I didn't buy the cigars, although I was thinking they'd be a nice gift for my friend Orestes back in the States. Of course she was right that it was most likely a rip-off, and in our circumstances we could ill afford to indulge every passing fancy. That was why we had traveled on a budget plan—although my original plan, instead of going on a honeymoon, was to stay in Bogotá and take care of all the paperwork for Silvia's visa. Not to worry, she said: her sister Clara could do it.

The Ring

That was when I first felt it. From heavenly bliss one evening to peremptory threats the next day, my joy was tempered by a vague hunch that I was missing part of the picture. And that was just the beginning. One day later we went to an island about a half-hour offshore, where the beach was postcard white and hotel staff grilled snacks for us all day. There was another American with a Colombian wife. As we frolicked in the turquoise water my wedding ring slipped off my finger and vanished into the sea, but I didn't notice until that evening.

We were dancing, again, at the hotel discothèque, and suddenly she said, "Where's your ring?" I was dismayed that it was missing, and we went upstairs to look for it— maybe I had dropped it washing my hands. I even removed the drain trap from the sink, but it wasn't there. However clearly upset I was myself for having lost it, Silvia mounted in indignation, rejected any explanation or atonement plea and, dismissing the relationship that the ring merely symbolized, also turned against a foundational value of our marriage: sex.

Cartagena was symptomatic in that every good or bad trait of our future together, and then apart, was prefigured in those five short days. The ring incident, I'm sure, contributed to my later sexual dysfunction, when she finally decided that she "felt like it," to which I could only reply, "Well, I guess my erection must be where the ring is, at the bottom of the sea." Silvia found the quip crude and disrespectful, and she was right: it was the first instance of my recourse to an increasingly mordant sarcasm with which I fended off her callous barbs.

We flew into Bogotá around noon. It was Thursday, and my flight home was the following morning. Silvia didn't have the keys to her apartment so we left our bags at the door while we tried to track down Verónica and Marcela, her two daughters. I suggested we go to the embassy to see about her visa, but once there we learned that it was an administrative workday and they were closed to the public. Not that it mattered: Clara had been unable to apostille the marriage certificate, because Silvia had given her a copy, not the original.

We'd skipped lunch, and Silvia started showing signs of disorientation. I suspected hypoglycemia because of the acute effects on her of a missed meal. We went to an American-style fast food joint nearby and waited half an hour for cold hamburgers. She regained her composure and we set out to make the best use of my remaining time in Bogotá, but accomplished nothing. We ended up at the home of her older sister, Norma, where we loitered until the girls showed up. Yet another sister, Isabel, joined us when she got off work.

There were six Cordero sisters. There had been a brother, but he died young. They were a tight-knit clan, intimately involved in each other's lives, acting almost interchangeably in the rearing of their young. Isabel, a nurse, treated the severe sunburn on my legs caused by the aloe lady rubbing away the sunscreen I had applied before she assaulted me. They relished the story, amused by my naïveté, augmented by Silvia's accounts of the cigar incident and our encounter with the seamy underside of Cartagena on our way to Guantánamo.

Guantánamo. They giggled at my sharp emphasis on the third-to-last syllable, and had me repeat it over and over. Bogotanos—*rolos*, as provincials call them—associate expressive diction with low breeding, and affect a stodgy monotone that marks them as the cold, pretentious elite the rest of the country holds them to be. As for me, I'd always loved proparoxytones and the rhythmic lilt they impart especially to verse, but I didn't mind humoring this mild mockery by my new family, and exaggerated my pronunciation to further amuse them.

Since they saw me as an American—a *gringo*—they condoned certain departures from their social mores; but even so, at times it was too much. The day of the wedding we had repaired to Norma's home for drinks, and when I crossed my legs on the sofa I heard a collective gasp. Later Silvia informed me privately that there was a hole in my shoe. The family was appalled at this telltale sign of improvidence, but all I could say was that they were very comfortable shoes and I hadn't noticed the hole. I gave them to Silvia and she threw them away.

The girls arrived and we had dinner. Marcela, especially, eyed me studiously, as if attempting to divine what kind of a man her mom had brought into their life. When Silvia woke up in the morning, Marcela was standing in the doorway, watching us spooned together as I still slept. She had never seen another man in her father's bed. We took a cab to the airport, stopping at a jewelry shop to buy a new ring. They even engraved it with our wedding date. Thoughts and feelings raced chaotically through my head as we parted. I had a wife now.

The months that followed became years, and they were pure limbo, or rather purgatory. As soon as I got home I began pressing for Silvia to provide me a key document needed to submit her visa petition. Some fellow was coming to the States and would bring it, she assured me. But when he arrived three months later he took another two to mail it from New York, and all she had sent was a copy of the certificate of marriage to her first husband, with a stamped handwritten note on the left margin that said they had divorced. I needed the actual decree.

Meantime, it was my duty, as her lawfully wedded husband, to afford her the lifestyle she felt entitled to, even though her ex was still munificent toward her and the daughters, because she never bothered to tell him she had remarried. Buying into her argument, I offered to send her one or two million pesos a month, which latter figure she held to when reminding me of my spousal duties, with persistent regularity. I wound up sending about $800 a month, midway between the two amounts in Colombian currency; therefore, she insisted, I was in default.

I continued to press for the decree but she started talking about a job opportunity with her friend Gloria, the director of a private foundation where Silvia had worked on and off over the years and, to hear it from her, had become a valued asset. Gloria was offering her a position at corporate headquarters in Spain, and Silvia was toying with the idea of going there on a work visa from the European Union instead of joining her new husband in the United States. The American Dream was overrated, she said, and I could always visit her in Madrid.

Eventually I got the fully legalized divorce decree for Silvia's first marriage, to Major Sergio Morales of the Colombian National Police—a man, she said, who had cheated on her from day one, and bestowed on her the distinction of bearing her first child within days of the next-door neighbor giving birth to a boy also sired by him. The neighbor was a close friend of Sergio's parents and visited them daily while Silvia lived there, so they could dote on their bastard grandson while the major was away chasing drug traffickers in the jungle.

Silvia's child, after all, was just a girl.

Sergio's dad was proud of the lad's exploits and pandered openly to his licentious ways. He himself would often boast of his own philandering, and according to Silvia her mother-in-law had dried up inside, embittered by her husband's constant public humiliation. The older Morales even attempted to insinuate himself on his nubile daughter-in-law and actually got her to sit on his knee one hot, sweaty afternoon. Someone told the major and he decided to move out of the paternal household before his wife became the mother of his siblings.

But he continued the family legacy of flaunting his infidelity in her face. At public establishments where they'd go to drink and be merry with his CNP buddies and their girlfriends and wives, he'd go dirty-dancing with easy women who'd walk right up to the table and ask him to the floor. Before long he would vanish with the floozy in the back, as his comrades laughed it off, assuring Silvia it was no big deal. The last straw, however, was when he seduced her niece Vicky, age sixteen. Divorcing him was the best thing Silvia ever did for herself.

Such accounts by her, in our constant conversations over the years, moved me both to pity and amusement, but I thought the catharsis she achieved by sharing them was preparing her for an honorable union with a man who could actually love her. Additionally her sexual inexperience, summarized in her laconic description of the major's monthly discharge of his conjugal obligations—mount, ejaculate, dismount and snore all night—made her prime material for a voyage of sexual discovery. I would make her my *lover;* I just knew.

In the early stages of the relationship I was charmed by her voracious interest in sex. She had to know *everything* and claimed that she'd been shortchanged by twenty years of marriage to a man who removed her from her parents' home at age sixteen and kept her in the dark about the pleasures that he himself reserved for the company of dishonest women, not to be shared with the "decent" wife who stayed home to watch the children, boss the maids around and pretty herself for when hubby got back from work, shaved and left again for the evening.

What a life, I thought. How *Colombian!* Yet far from imagining the blowback effect of this on our relationship, I thought it would increase Silvia's interest in the benefits of a fair partnership, both giving and receiving in equal measure, each one's freedom limited only by an appreciation for the other's rights, a sensitivity to each other's feelings. She would be loyal to a man that respected her, passionate in her commitment to a partner who could assure her unconditional love and fidelity, something she had never had before.

Simple.

But her sexual awakening went beyond that. After her divorce she fell in with a group of "modern" females who spent hours at the gym keeping in shape to better their chances of a Good Catch. Adriana, whom Silvia considered her best friend, was the best example of this approach. At any given time she'd be "hooked up" with two or three *gringos* she met at nightspots frequented by Special Forces jocks on temporary duty with the embassy. Mark had promised to marry her, but disappeared. Ted, however, paid her way through beauty school.

She was a knockout, to be sure: jet-black hair flowing freely to the waist and near-Asian facial features on a tall, lithe, deep amber body, upgraded by monomaniacal exercise and breast augmentation. A true "exotic"—though I didn't think much of her ass when I met her later. By Silvia's account, a nymphomaniac, too, unable to resist the advances of any decent-looking male even if his bank account didn't justify a long-term relationship. The gym was rife with gossip of men who couldn't keep up with her when she took them home for sex.

Adriana sparked Silvia's interest in sodomy. It wasn't new to me, after all the naughty girls I had dated in college, but my interest in this venerable Greco-Roman tradition was mild at best—vaginas had always seemed to me perfectly adequate. Yet I had no serious objection to it, morally or otherwise, and indulged Silvia by researching it and reporting to her my findings. As a widespread means of gratification among gay men, I assumed there had to be something about phallic suffusion of the rectum that was getting all the buzz. Silvia listened with rapt attention, and we promised each other to try it.

Our sex talks during this prenuptial friendship stage were earnest and diligent. There was an aimless period of my life during which I endured the lusty enthusiasm of young college girls in the throes of the seventies' sexual revolution. I had dropped out of architecture school in Colombia and came to the States to try my luck, but got stuck for a while in a hedonistic rut. Silvia was in thrall of my bawdy experiences, and recounting them gave me a rise, too. The stories served as scripts for extended sessions of international phone sex.

This melding of our imaginations was a delightful pastime, and we were on the phone every day. Adriana had a vibrator and Silvia wanted one, too, so I mailed her a Hitachi HV-250R... the Cadillac of self-gratification, according to the reviews. It had two power settings, but Silvia never used high, because it hurt her. She had a way of drifting out of other topics and steering conversation to the matter at hand, which I could hear humming in the background. She'd answer anything I said with a husky "Uh-huh," and I knew it was time to say something else.

She became addicted to my voice. It was both soothing and exciting to her as a ritual element of our life apart; but also, perhaps, because she could separate it from its source and apply it as a soundtrack to her own personal fantasies. She couldn't fall asleep unless she heard it, she said. Most nights I would tuck her in with the aid of Simón, our mechanical friend (so named after Colombian independence hero Simón Bolívar, *El Libertador*), who eased her transition from sexual fantasy, through multiple orgasms, to sweet dreams. I wasn't surprised, when we started sleeping together, to find that she sucked her thumb.

But it wasn't just sex. "Have you ever listened to Mozart?" she asked me one Sunday morning (I'd call early on weekends because I had free minutes). "Yes, I've listened to Mozart all my life." She liked that: "Mozart and Bach make me feel like I have wings and I can fly up to heaven," she said. I could hardly believe it: Mozart's nimble charm; Bach's cosmic explorations; Beethoven—behemoth and leviathan all at once, implacable juggernaut... we could have all *that!*

And that's what it was, really: a quest for convergence, for the reconciliation of opposites, the sublime and the profane, body and soul. We cultivated a nuanced ethos that rejected taboos as obstacles to knowledge, and every source was valid in our search for meaning, freedom and transcendence. The later decay of the relationship made clear that she didn't quite see it the same way I did, or perhaps we strayed apart over time; but Silvia put it best one day when I chided her about the heavy sexual content of our colloquia: "It's all culture."

I couldn't agree more. My struggle for understanding had been characterized since childhood by an intractable conflict between the urges of the senses and a sense of moral duty. My daily communion in Catholic school became an equally fervent rejection of the Church when I discovered masturbation (my confessor seemed a bit too interested in the details). And yet I so over-intellectualized my approaches to the opposite sex that I remained a virgin until age twenty. I didn't get it when it came to women; when they finally came to me, I overcompensated. This time I was determined to get it right.

Cheat Chat

Our first encounter had been inauspicious. I found Silvia in one of those Internet matchmaking sites, and was drawn to the soulful, pensive expression of her profile snapshot: the look of suppressed desire. I referred to her as "doe-eyed" but she didn't appreciate the comparison to wildlife. Maybe she'd never seen *Bambi*, I mused. I left it at that for a while, but approached her again a few months later, and asked if she remembered me. "Yes, you're the guy who called me a moose." She was being wicked, of course, but I liked it. We had game.

I was still reeling from a misguided infatuation I'd fallen into after years of single fatherhood following a messy divorce. My heartstrings were astir, having theretofore suppressed any desire for intimacy and companionship in order to dedicate my full attention to my children when their mother jumped ship. When I reconnected with Silvia, she was exploring a relationship with a Spanish art dealer who had met her the same way I had. We e-mailed back and forth, sharing hopes and disappointments, and a comfortable familiarity began to grow.

She would always inquire about Graciela, the object of my delusion, a young and talented musician who'd shown an extraordinary commitment to Chris and Lizzie when I was faced with the prospect of raising them alone. They were her students, and our collaboration grew into an ambitious project to assemble young musicians from around the world, at yearly concerts that I helped her organize. We traveled together, and spent more time with each other than she did with her boorish, unappreciative husband. I fell for her, and it was a disaster.

I would ask Silvia about Víctor, the Spaniard who pursued her. She consulted me about various issues in their budding romance, about which something was fishy. We had graduated to real-time conversations on chat media, that she would cut short when it was time to get on line with her "boyfriend," as she was calling him already. They chatted regularly around 8:00 pm my time, or 2:00 am in Spain. Víctor was burning the midnight oil to woo this pretty Colombian divorcée. But how come he always showed up right after she signed in?

I didn't want to seem cynical, but she asked, so I ventured a guess: he would block her until he saw her come on line, and then unblock her for their "date." Thus he made it seem like *she* was chasing *him,* and could hide from her other online conversations he might be having. I suggested that she give him a taste of his own medicine. We tested the technique and she was exultant at her new-found power. He would finally cave in and log on much after the appointed time, asking why *she* was "late" when she joined him. She had turned the tables, with my help.

A sneaky complicity ensued. Víctor's days were numbered, because there was a fundamental dishonesty in his dealings with Silvia. But she clung to the illusion and insisted that these minor issues would work themselves out over time. She continued to share her misgivings down to the most intimate details, and yet she couldn't wait to meet him. Eventually he announced a trip to Bogotá, on account of certain business interests that required his personal attention. When last we talked she was ecstatic; then she dropped out of sight for over a month.

I got home from a job in Washington one day, and there was e-mail from Silvia: "Log on tonight. I need to talk to you." She was in a frightful state. It was over. He was nothing like she thought he was. She was disconsolate, desperate, a wreck. "Give me your phone number," I wrote. "I'll call you." And then I heard her voice for the first time: delicate, childlike and—though I knew she was in pain, I couldn't help but notice—sexy. She was sobbing, rambling uncontrollably, trying to tell the story from all ends at once. As best I could, I soothed her.

After that evening we stopped chatting on line and were always on the phone. As she added details, the Víctor affair became increasingly amusing, which I made no effort to conceal. She vested her full trust in me, and soon she was laughing about it, too. The Spaniard took her to artsy gatherings as eye candy, to show her off. The flattery and attention would arouse her and she wanted to throw herself at him and have wild sex as soon as they got home—but first he had to put away his metrosexual wardrobe, fold his trousers, hang his shirt.

He had a sizable penis and at first she had a hard time fitting it in her petite vagina, unaffected by childbirth because her children were both delivered by Caesarian section. Eventually she got the hang of it and really liked it, but as he came he would always pull out and spoot all over her. She asked me if that was normal and I said yes... in porn films. Before they met he'd been extolling the goodness of sex toys, describing their use, and promised to bring some. She was piqued, but he arrived empty-handed—not even a measly dildo.

"What a disappointment," I chuckled, taking note of the kind of favors that would get her attention. But most of all, in all those months of online chatting, he never mentioned to her a certain physical deformity. She was shocked when she saw it as soon as he emerged from the airport gate, but wings of love got her over the hump. Later, though, she said she could feel him sapping her "energy," draining her life force as they lay in bed together, until she finally wound up in the hospital for a week. She never did say what the exact diagnosis was.

This, I thought, was weird. But so were many other stories she told me. The final straw was an incident at an ATM. As he was entering his PIN, he turned around to block her view of the keypad. "With his hump?" I asked politely. "Oh, stop it!" she giggled; she wasn't trying to steal his PIN, but only to get up closer and cuddle—Bogotá can get pretty cold at night. "Besides," she added, "what need had I to steal from him? He kept a bag in the apartment with fifty million pesos cash. He said I could take as much as I wanted, whenever I wanted, and I never did."

Then why stop at an ATM? Such questions often drifted into my mind, but I dismissed them as petty quibbles; you can't love and distrust at the same time. But Víctor distrusted her, which led to her blowing up and breaking up with him on the spot. She did show up the next day at the apartment he was renting in a well-to-do part of town, to pick up her things. She expected him to give her one last try, to apologize, to say that he loved her. Instead, he told her that if she had any pride she wouldn't have bothered to return, and asked for the key.

That's probably when she e-mailed me. She had to purge her demons, to convince herself that she had done the right thing, that she was blameless and he was a jerk. I couldn't know otherwise so I played along, plus I'd been waiting for a chance to go into action. Over the following weeks she vented her frustration over the failed relationship, and pored over detailed memories of everything that was wrong with it. I helped her digest lessons from the experience, and gently but surely reeled her in... or was it the other way around?

Soon we were discussing the nature of sexual attraction and its role in a serious relationship, the advantages of monogamy versus promiscuity, the meaning of love, and many such heady matters. But above all she wanted to pick my brain in the area of sexual practices and techniques, which I was glad to share with her as far as I knew, or research if I didn't. One evening I asked her if she wouldn't mind pretending to have sex with me so that I could bring myself to climax, aroused by our conversation. I faked it, but she was hooked, as I intended.

Eventually we decided it was time to meet. It had been barely a year since her Spanish fling went flat, but we were already talking love, with an emphasis on sex. I felt it was important to stay focused on what mattered most to both of us, carefully avoiding any false dichotomy between physical and spiritual attraction, because I considered erotic tension an important means of strengthening emotional bonds. But all of this verbal intimacy would become no more than a stultifying exercise in futility if we didn't bring it to fruition soon.

A few days before I left to meet her I spent the afternoon at a Washington record store assembling a representative sampling of the classical universe, with the eager assistance of a music student working the register, who joined me in my quest for the best of the best, for two hundred dollars or less. I got about a dozen CDs encompassing some of the most compelling sonatas, cantatas, concertos, symphonies and chamber music I could think of. I was looking to frame our encounter in the highest possible terms of reference.

Bogotá

I booked a suite in a small boutique hotel just off 93rd Street, a fashionable restaurant and entertainment district in Bogotá, frequented by mamas' boys in BMWs and silicone-laden Barbie dolls, none of which I was aware of until I got there. Reviewing the options over the Internet it just seemed a cozy little place to make our first acquaintance, with fresh, modern décor and reasonable rates, surprisingly, for the area. I told the kids I had an out-of-town assignment, left them with their mother and got on an airplane to Colombia for the ride of my life.

At the airport, Silvia was waiting just outside the gate, standing next to her sister Catalina, who looked just like her. Isabel was also there. I made a beeline straight to Silvia, confounding her devious scheme to confuse me, and introduced myself politely, with a handshake, avoiding all presumption. We'd been talking for two years, but we hadn't truly met and I wanted to allow the encounter to sink in. How could I know she'd feel as comfortable in person as we had been over countless hours of long-distance conversation, however intimate?

The sisters came with us to the hotel, which the cabby took about half an hour to find because I forgot to bring the address. All six eyes were glued on me during check-in, keen to the relaxed bonhomie with which I addressed the hotel staff and asked if they had any decent wine. It was late and the restaurant was closed, but they let us in to see their stock: there were several nice reds from Chile and Argentina. I also asked if the room had a sound system, which it didn't, but they loaned us a boom box that we took upstairs to play Silvia's new CDs.

So far I seemed to be making a good impression, which was easy because I was buoyant with the excitement of meeting her, plus several in-flight Bloody Marys. She sat in the farthest armchair across the room; Isabel and Catalina sat on the couch, closer to me, as I poured them wine and started the music. Silvia hardly spoke, but observed with fierce intensity as I interacted with her older sisters. Clearly, I had to win them over. Good thing they had a sense of humor; they laughed over my antics as I tried to recover from tripping over the coffee table and said something ridiculous to save face.

After two bottles Catalina wanted to leave but Isabel, tipsy, wanted to order another one. Catalina insisted that they should give us some space for further acquaintance, but I diffused the awkward moment by suggesting that they go home together and we could reconvene in the morning to make plans. I'd been traveling all day and needed some rest, I explained. The phone rang at two-thirty in the morning. It was Silvia: "I knew that I would like you, Daniel, but I never imagined I'd like you so much." It was working, I thought, and slept like a baby.

I called around ten and we agreed to meet at her apartment, a fifth-floor walk-up in a slightly dingy part of Bogotá. She was alone. Verónica and Marcela were away for the holidays with their dad in Cúcuta, on the Venezuelan border. There was a coy politeness, as we were already quite intimate on a verbal basis, but had yet to approach one another physically. I bore gifts, and she wanted to see them right away. There was a childlike sparkle in her eyes as she opened each package. They were *sooo* beautiful, she squealed, smiling brightly.

And so they were. Although I'd already shipped her several gifts (including Simón), I had also hoarded a few: mainly delicate, exotic lingerie by the likes of La Perla, Aubade and I.D. Sarrieri. It's not that I spared no expense when it came to fueling sexual fantasy; I just didn't keep track—the collection represented a small fortune. We had already discussed the importance of erotic tension and agreed it was about fifty-one percent of a meaningful relationship; it carried quorum. So I never felt bad about sexing her up, and these tasteful, high-end props really did the trick.

She chose to wear a crimson Simone Pérèle bustier top that complemented both her hair and skin tone. I took pictures of her modeling it before a mirror. In one lucky shot her reddish hair was backlit by reflected flash; she seemed to glow from within, her mirror image smiling with approval from the other side. As she admired herself I came to her from behind and kissed her lightly at the turn from neck to shoulder. She viewed me from the mirror in breathless anticipation, unsure if we were going to "do it" then and there. But I let the tension build.

"Your sisters are expecting us," I teased her, and she snapped out of it.

"Oh, right! We've got to go."

There was time; I was there only to see her, I reminded her, unlike Víctor, who had fit her in as a sideline to his "business trip." He just wanted to sound important, but he had made a big mistake. I wanted to meet her friends, her family, to insert myself in her everyday life. I wanted her entire existence to be a part of mine, for our shared experiences to be firmly grounded in reality. I wanted to fall in love with her... or maybe I already had.

Lipo Sucks

Apparently my goofy soirée with Catalina and Isabel had been a hit; they organized a noontime welcome party at the home of yet another sister, Elsa, the youngest. They had about three kids each so there were over a dozen when we got there, plus two husbands and a couple of family friends. Lunch was late, so Silvia slipped away with me to a nearby upscale mall, where I got a haircut and she a manicure, topped off by a two-tone French enamel job. She wanted me to get a manicure, too, but I demurred.

"I'm not Víctor," I reminded her.

On the way back we stopped at a huge Carrefour, part of a French supermarket chain that had invaded Colombia since the last time I had been there. There was a good Malbec from Mendoza for under ten dollars, so we took a couple of bottles. Lunch was ready and the atmosphere was sprightly, children all over me, people old and young dancing to salsa, cumbia and vallenato music coming from a beat-up boom box on a corner chair. You can't put Colombians together for any length of time without a dance party breaking out.

The wine was gone in no time, and I was reminded of the wedding feast at Cana. In lieu of supernatural powers, though, I gave a hundred-dollar bill to a couple of the older kids and sent them to Carrefour for as many bottles as the cash would get them. They found the Malbec but bought an older, pricier vintage, so they came back with only seven bottles—still a pretty good deal. Silvia eyed me intently from across the room, exuding a sultry allure that froze the scene and threw me off track of several conversations I had going at the same time.

"Let's go," she signaled.

On the way to my place, we stopped at *Salto del Angel,* a chichi 93rd Street club. Colombia has superb architecture—bold, imaginative, with agile, playful spaces—and this was a good example. We sat in a mezzanine cantilevered into the dance floor under a soaring skylight held up by textured columns that made light of their structural duties. I had always liked the technique of casting concrete into forms lined with *peine de mono* (Apeiba aspera), a soft, coarse wood that leaves a rugged, organic look when burned off the dry cement.

I wasn't hungry, so I ordered *seviche* from the appetizer menu. It had a surprising touch of mango, a clever update to the ubiquitous South American standby. We danced a little, but the music was too glitzy, "American," for my taste, and we returned to the table. Silvia, who'd ordered nothing, ate most of my *seviche*. She pointed out a *telenovela* actress seated at a large table with a well-dressed group by the dance floor. I picked up that the joint was a celebrity-studded hot spot and shrugged, underwhelmed.

"You know, when I came here with Víctor, they turned him back at the door," she said. I hadn't noticed the bouncers on our way in. "It sounds to me like they turned *both* of you away," I answered mentally, hoping that she wasn't telepathically on to my inner sarcasm. "He was furious," she continued. "He was telling them, 'Don't you know who I am?' " In the same vein as my earlier answer, I thought, "Maybe they *did.*" The frivolous chitchat was beginning to annoy me, when she said, "I don't even have to make love to you to feel a special magic just being together."

Whatever she meant by that, it was awfully put. "Well, I guess I made a mistake," I said, rising to leave. "Come on, I'll get you a cab." If this was to become a high-school tease, I'd cut it short at once. I still had time to fly down to Cali and spend it with friends and family. "What's wrong, Daniel?" she asked. "Why are you upset?" I said, "Silvia, I didn't come all the way from Washington just to get laid. If you think that you're going to use sex to manipulate me, we're off to a very bad start." She was shocked: "But I *want* to make love to you. I want to fuck you right now."

Much better, I thought. But the sex was awful. I had helped her pay for a liposuction procedure to remove some of the midriff flab that mortified her. She was still recovering and had to wear a tight girdle with a wide crotch that blocked access to her vagina. On top of which she insisted there was "something wrong" with said vagina, because it was inordinately resistant to penetration. I'd heard the story several times and took it with a grain of salt, confident that a little elbow grease and a fine German lubricant I brought along would do the trick.

It was torture, though. The stiff girdle crotch rubbed coarsely against one side of my penis, and my erection began to flag after repeated attempts to get past her inner labia, clamped shut like a bear trap. Arousal gave way to frustration but the doctor had warned her against removing the girdle, so the upgrade that was supposed to make her sexier prevented her, in fact, from having sex. She whimpered apologetically and we persevered dutifully in the endeavor: full entry was achieved around three-thirty in the morning.

Breakfast was spectacular downstairs; I hadn't realized it was included. Silvia was aglow, although still somewhat embarrassed, and she leapt gleefully at my suggestion that we go shopping for a girdle with a snap-open crotch. We found one downtown and got another one for Isabel, who'd just had the same procedure, because the clinic where she worked gave her a discount. I wanted to survey women in the street to find out if any of them *hadn't* had some kind of plastic surgery, but we had homework so we ran back to the hotel.

   She got out of the Nazi girdle and I saw her completely naked for the first time. Her lower back and ribcage were bruised by the adipose extraction, and her skin hadn't quite set in place; I could see why the girdle was necessary. The suite had a nice Jacuzzi that we slipped into with a fresh bottle of wine, seeking through soft conversation and gentle physical approaches, sweet kisses and caresses, to smooth out the (literally) grating experience from our first sally. She invited me to bed. "And the girdle?" I asked. "Later," she replied, brushing it aside.

   Our lovemaking got better over successive sessions, nonstop over the next three days. Her body began responding more naturally, intuitively, to the rhythmic beckoning of mine, her instincts gradually overcoming her misgivings. Soon she was taking the initiative and I was gratified to see her kinetic self-assurance when on top; I merely had to modulate pressure and speed ever so slightly to stay on the edge, hardly doing anything myself. I began to see what I had come to find: a new aesthetic paradigm of unrestrained sensuality, erotic grace.

"That's a fine little motor you've got there," I'd tease her, pointing to her pelvis as she continued to refine her stroke, hips and waist in counter-rhythmic syncopation. She smiled and gasped simultaneously, doubly challenged by the separate tasks of awakening to a growing intensity of pleasure while grappling with the metaphysical dimensions of the physical act. Around noon one day it struck me, as her bottom swiveled entirely from the hip, upper frame delicately balanced in perfect alignment with the vertical shaft running smoothly through the glistening, dewy rosebud that her labia had blossomed into, how right I'd been about that first photograph.

"You've made me such a slut," she'd moan as I plunged into her with deep, earnest intent. I wasn't used to "talking dirty" in bed, but from her it sounded right: it was an "excited utterance," forthright and plain. It got me to thinking that all women should want that, a mutual transparency of body and mind, and be free to feel that way in the company of a trusted partner, a *lover*. Where did we always go wrong? Why did one always have to imprison another, attach all kinds of alien contingencies to this highest, most abstract yet concrete state of being? Why was there always a *price?*

On the third day I started feeling incredibly hungry, hungrier than I remembered ever being. We hadn't left the room, or allowed the chambermaids to clean it. "Later," Silvia said every time it came up. But it was my last full day in Bogotá and I wanted to get Lizzie an earring set of genuine Muzo emeralds, the finest in the world. We had another hotel breakfast and headed downtown, to the corner of Seventh and Jiménez, the heart of the emerald district. Silvia's haggling skills were impressive: we got a gorgeous pair and had them set in 18-karat gold.

That was the last nice thing she ever did for my daughter. An irrational resentment began to build and the mere mention of Lizzie would send Silvia into a rage. We strolled downtown as the goldsmith finished the earrings in a tiny fourth-floor shop behind a heavy, barred steel door. Silvia's entire family thought poorly of the downtown area and hardly ever ventured there, but I had always been drawn to its earthy matter-of-factness... though it's true that in 1983 I had witnessed a gunfight right in the middle of Tenth Avenue.

The earrings were superb.

We had lunch at a rooftop restaurant in the hillside Candelaria district, where many colonial-era buildings still stand. The nearby Basilica of the Immaculate Conception dominated a breathtaking view of the city. The mood was breezy and romantic, but the fish wasn't very good. Silvia made arrangements with Elsa and her husband Pedro to go out that evening. I wanted to take them to a steakhouse that I'd used to frequent when I'd lived in Bogotá a quarter-century earlier. I wondered if it was still there, and where exactly "there" was.

"Here It Is" (*Aquí Es*) was the actual *name* of the establishment, so we knew exactly where we were when we got there. Unlike the foppish pretentiousness of the Candelaria joint, this was a high-value proposition: beer-marinated beef heaped high on tin trays, with generous sides of salt-boiled potato and grilled corn-on-the-cob, which they call *choclo.* For a little extra there was also a drop-dead guacamole, chunky and with lots of onion. I stepped outside for a smoke and bought a red rose for Silvia from a sidewalk vendor. She'd always remember that.

On the way home she sat beside me in the back seat, holding the flower. She started running her fingers softly up and down my nape and I could feel myself drifting off, into a reverie that I wanted never to return from. Pedro and Elsa quipped that she had tamed me, because I looked like a puppy, and it was true: I felt like one, too. The ride was almost an hour, but I wished it would never end. Even after days of uninhibited sex play, this was the closest I had felt to her yet. During that cab ride from the steakhouse to our hotel, I decided I wanted to marry her.

I didn't tell her right away, though; with so much pending prolegomena, I'd be selling myself short. We lingered briefly at the hotel. It was a cold, drizzly night, more like the Bogotá I remembered from the seventies, before the recent warming trend. There was a fireplace in the suite and we hadn't used it, nor knew how. They sent up some synthetic fire logs, which, when lit, oozed oily drops of blue liquid fire that walked spookily along the hearth and filled the room with rancid black smoke. "That's no fireplace!" I cried. "It's a fucking volcano!"

We scrambled to open the windows and balcony doors as hotel staff ran to the rescue. The flue was clogged and the logs, clearly, completely useless. The room was uninhabitable and we gasped and wheezed, waiting for staff to slay the dragon, that kept coming back like those annoying birthday candles. Meekly apologetic, the night manager offered to bring in fans.

"How about we go dancing?" suggested Pedro, his eyes, and ours, watery both from the smoke and the raucous laughter we were rolling in. He knew of a disco on 88th Street.

As we crossed Tenth Avenue a man was walking toward us up the hill, backlit by the street lights below, carrying what looked to me, in silhouette, like a chicken dangling from its feet—a common sight when I was growing up in Tuluá, riding the bus to Cali. As he came near I realized that it was a half-open collapsible umbrella. Startled by the vivid optical illusion, I told the others what I thought I'd seen, now that they could see what it really was. For Silvia, though, the point was my original misperception, not the later shock of cognitive correction.

A subtle distinction, to be sure, but it bugged me that she missed it. Her take, however, was still, to her, so funny that she almost wet her Sarrieris, and whenever she saw another umbrella she'd say, "Look, a chicken!" and again burst out in laughter. My observation wasn't meant as a joke at all, but she was so amused that I joined in the fun, adding descriptors to the various kinds of "chickens" we encountered along the way. No matter how hard we tried to hold it in, we chortled constantly until we got to 88th Street. The club wasn't there.

Wending our way back to 93rd Street we came across a seedy little joint on 91st, which is more of an alley than a street. *Salomé,* read the sign over the door, whence issued the musky mango tones and complex, polyrhythmic syncopation of the legendary Sonora Matancera, an orchestra I had learned to love during my college years in Cali. The Sonora was the most brilliant, accomplished product of the golden age of Cuban *son.* We stayed, and the table was soon stocked with rum and Coca-Cola, the only proper drink under the circumstances.

Silvia could *so* do *son.* She wasn't very familiar with it but her every muscle seemed to lock on to the dynamic flow dictated by the music. I couldn't remember, in fact, having ever danced so freely with anyone *since* college. The owner collected *son* and classic salsa, and we feasted our senses on the edgy hits of Richie Ray, Eddie Palmieri and other

Afro-Caribbean/Jazz fusion pioneers that he had on vinyl. Pedro had a choppy, *rolo* version of high-stepping salsa that he'd learned in Cali when he'd lived there briefly in the nineties. We stayed till closing.

Silvia and I didn't get much sleep when we got back to the room, where two industrial air extractors struggled in vain to remove the acrid vestiges of the fireplace eruption. She was passionate, and we didn't so much fall asleep as spend ourselves into oblivion in the discharge of our fierce arousal. Barely an hour later it was time to go, and I surprised her by assailing her still-engorged vagina yet again with lips and tongue already raw from several days of hard work. My parting shot gushed into her sideways as she lay in figure four across the bed.

We ran out of time and I got up to make my bags, but Silvia pushed me aside— she was an expert packer and was done before I knew it. We had to skip breakfast and headed straight to the airport, where we waited in line almost two hours just to get up to the ticket counter. We touched and nuzzled affectionately, addressing only obliquely the question of what next. Everything was different now, we realized, and neither one of us wanted to force the issue. But we liked being together. As I buckled in and the plane lifted off to Washington, I was happy.

The Wedding

"You never fucked my ass," was the first thing she said when we got on the phone that evening. I was embarrassed, because I'd given her my word, but she laughed it off: "Now we have to see each other again." I agreed, and we began discussing options. Our first idea was that she simply come up stateside on a tourist visa, fuck some more, look around. I always compared lovers to dancers: when you see a really good couple on the floor, it's because they dance regularly together and have rapport. Sex, too, gets better over time, and may grow, I believed, into a love that keeps on growing.

As in any other language—Spanish or French, music or math—there's always room for learning, to acquire fluency by practice, mastery by inspiration. Whether prose or poetry, from the symphonic sweep of an all-night romp to the light divertimento of a morning quickie, each event has a unique character and distinct meaning, its own place in the story of life, in the hierarchy of memory; each a moment of convergence for two existences to become one, a single being together. Or so, at least, I always thought—a comforting illusion, perhaps.

Silvia didn't get the visa, because I told her to be truthful at the interview. So they asked her if her sponsor was her boyfriend, and she said yes. Then they asked her if we planned to marry, and she said yes. Then they told her, "Wayell, ma'am, y'all din' applah fer thuh raht kahnd a' veesa. Y'all has to eyethur applah fer a fiauncey veesa an' marry up'air, or marry down heer an' *then* go up'air, or vicee-versy." I didn't actually know if she talked like that, but I hated the meddlesome bitch that stood between us, and fancied her an Appalachian hillbilly.

This made things harder, but difficulty always hardened my resolve. After consulting with an immigration lawyer I was acquainted with from interpreting at DC Superior Court, it appeared that marrying Silvia in Colombia and then applying for her as a spouse was a quicker path to reunion than getting in line for a fiancée visa. Plus the indeterminacy of the latter made me fear that she'd get cold feet after a while and go running back home.

I was aware of the daunting effect of culture shock—better to burn the ships, like Cortés.

The prospect of becoming husband and wife fueled a new sense of intimacy, but something else surfaced that I hadn't noticed before: Silvia's misgivings about my financial solvency. I'd been rather grand with her, showering her with gifts and flowers on special occasions, and occasionally for no reason at all. But I'd also confided (in retrospect, not a good idea) that I sometimes ran aground between assignments, and that my financial skills were quite nearly nonexistent. At the end of my Bogotá visit, for instance, all I had was twenty dollars.

I tried to convey to her my deep-seated trust in destiny, perhaps a lingering after-effect of my Catholic upbringing: "God will provide," we were always told. My own corollary was that where there's love, all else follows. She was adamant, however, in the opposite: "You cannot live on love alone," she'd always go back to, in spite of her credentials as a rosary-praying Catholic—she knew the sacred mysteries for each day of the week. She also took regular communion, though she wasn't a big fan of confession: "God already knows," was her excuse.

I'd built a good reputation among Washington conference interpreters, and there was no shortage of assignments, although neither was there any regularity. The international organizations I usually worked for had become good clients, but the dry spells could last for weeks, and I was never prepared for them. I'd lived like that for years, but Silvia just couldn't see it, and didn't share my faith in divine providence. From a practical point of view, marrying me didn't make a lot of sense—but suddenly fortune smiled on me... or sort of smirked a little.

The International Monetary Fund was looking for a translator and, even though I'd worked almost exclusively as an interpreter for over a decade, I had started out as a translator and had the skills to compete for this position on one of the strongest translation teams in Washington. They took me on for a three-month trial period, by the end of which I was coordinating projects with contractors in other countries. Silvia and I planned to marry in late April, but the IMF asked me to stay another two weeks so we moved the wedding to May.

Around then, however, Venezuelan strongman Hugo Chávez paid off Argentina's debt with the IMF, whose operating budget is funded from debt service, and the resulting cash crunch led to a hiring freeze that landed me back on the cold streets of the freelance interpreting market. Thanks, Hugo. Being optimistic about the job, I hadn't been too prudent with the handsome salary I was drawing in the meantime, so my pockets weren't the deepest when I boarded an airplane again to Bogotá, though I carried gifts for the entire Cordero clan.

This time Verónica and Marcela were home, and I undertook gingerly to befriend them, aware of their sour experience with Víctor. I spent the first night in the guest room, as we weren't married yet and it would have been improper to sleep together, at least in this *rolo* household. Silvia came to tuck me in and I ripped a plaid flannel miniskirt I'd brought her, in my zeal to mount her on the sofa bed while the girls were at the store. During the tussle a spring popped out of the folding frame and the mattress sagged dismally as we came.

The girls had midterms, so they couldn't make it to the wedding. Adriana and Pilar, Silvia's other merry girlfriend, came to help her get in gear for the ceremony to be held at a downtown Notary Public. Such offices have similar functions, in Colombia, to a Magistrate or Justice of the Peace in the U.S. It was my first close-up view of Adriana, whose sex appeal Silvia had made much of, and in spite of rather weak hindquarters she did indeed pack a heavy testosterone wallop. She was a bit virile, in fact, and, as Silvia also noted, conversationally inept.

I knew that second wedding dresses aren't supposed to be white, but was flummoxed by Silvia's choice of a bright teal slant-hem, bodiced two-piece she had made herself for the occasion. It was the weirdest dress a woman ever wore to marry me—but I'd only married once before, so what did I know. Her friends were busy (at the gym, no doubt) and would meet us later. Silvia's look-alike sister Catalina was our witness and wedding photographer at Notary Public 64. There was a small ceremony hall with cheesy, primitivist landscapes on the wall.

The tenderfoot lawyer Silvia had hired to iron out the legal wrinkles looked on somberly as the Notary Public, a jovial, affable man in his sixties, guided us through the formalities of the brief event. Catalina was Vicky's mother, and I wondered what might be going through her mind at her sister's second wedding after what she'd been through with Sergio and her daughter. Or did she know? The family had a *rolo* way of sweeping things under the rug. All such queer circumstances notwithstanding, I had a clear sense that destiny was fully in charge.

Pilar did join us at the Notary Public's, but the ceremony was over and we were waiting for the certificate. I handed the lawyer 600,000 pesos cash—about $300—the balance of what we owed him for his services, and he smiled for the first time all morning. We had lunch at a sushi place not far from Silvia's apartment and I asked for wasabe, but they'd never heard of it so they brought us some sort of mayonnaise instead. We made arrangements at a nearby Chinese restaurant for an evening dinner for family and friends.

Norma had asked us over and we walked into a minefield of supercharged kids all wanting to know if they could call me uncle. I lifted them up to a ceiling rafter and took pictures of them hanging in a row like possums. Before long, they *were* crying uncle. I wanted to see the pictures, but Norma never developed the film, which I left with her hoping to get it printed faster. One of the kids was Vicky's four-year-old boy. She'd married a military attaché to the Colombian embassy in Stockholm, but the boy's age dated him to the time of Silvia's divorce.

Neighbors, friends and family kept dropping in to take a look at the *gringo* Silvia had married, and were surprised—disappointed?—that I could communicate in perfect Spanish—as well, even, as *rolos* presume to speak it themselves. Vicky showed up and stared at me sullenly, without so much as a perfunctory greeting. She wouldn't take her eyes off me, in fact. I surmised that there was more to her story than I knew, but I was in a jolly mood so I ignored her, working the crowd with the easy aplomb of an old ham. And then I crossed my legs...

Some thirty guests showed up for dinner. Again we ran out of wine and sent for more. Verónica took over as wedding photographer and became very fond of my trusty old Nikon. I thought to give it to her but I still needed it, so I'd get her one later, I figured. Pilar showed up late again with her latest boyfriend, a prominent architect, married and with children. Silvia's sisters frowned on the company she kept and rebuked her for preferring them to family. She had always been the most aloof of the Cordero girls, and they resented it.

The crowd dropped away in ones and twos and threes. Verónica and Marcela followed their cousins to a late-night movie party at Catalina's.

"Tonight we sleep in my bed," Silvia beamed, and she kissed me as I'd taught her, mouth half-open at a quarter turn to mine. She dropped on her back in the middle of the bed, thighs spread high and wide to receive me.

"No," she whispered, as my cock touched her outer labia. "I want it in my ass."

I lowered my aim the crucial half-inch difference to our higher purpose.

"Aahhh," she breathed. "At last."

The girls never made it home and we had an early flight. Silvia had us packed in no time. We took a taxi to the airport, boarded our plane, fastened our seatbelts and were off to Cartagena. The proud sixteenth-century city that had withstood brutal sieges by the English, centuries of pillage by bloodthirsty pirates and corsairs, and was host to the ghastly inhumanity of the slave trade, would now welcome within its fortress walls, standing watch over Columbus's Caribbean, the happiest couple in the world.

The Wait

During the wait for Silvia's visa Norma asked me for a favor. I'd helped them with a family tourist visa, and her oldest son Mario had already spent some time in Miami working at a restaurant to help himself through college. Now Héctor, her husband, was on his way, and she wanted to know if I could put him up while he looked for work in the Washington area. He got lost exiting the baggage claim area (not an easy thing to do) but I found him and took him with me into DC the next day. Some people I'd met in court were in the catering business and I tried to connect him.

Eventually he landed a construction job with a *chueco* work permit—a cloak-and-dagger illegal document purchase that put me at some risk one evening in the Adams Morgan district of Washington—and started generating income for the Cordero clan. I provided free housing and transportation, plus fairly frequent meals on the house, so his financial deployment appeared to be successful. Héctor was something of a simpleton, yet we became good friends. I liked cooking for him, because he earnestly enjoyed my meatloaf, my salads, my stew.

He was *so* out of place, though, completely unable to grasp the reality of being in another country. "They actually leave cars out in the lot, unattended, at night?" he asked me as we walked by a car dealership one evening. Apparently that was inconceivable in Colombia. "Well, it's nighttime, and the cars are out in the lot, unattended," I pointed out, sarcastically. "What do you think?" He had an agreement with Norma: if either could marry for a green card, they'd then divorce and send for the other. But he was homesick, and blew a date with a potential bride.

My mother, a German-American still living in Colombia after my dad died in 1999, was coming to visit in May. With summer vacations coming up and my children in the house all day while I was away, I asked Héctor to find other accommodations, because my ex would surely find a way to twist the situation into a custody issue. Also, I needed the room for my mom. When she arrived she continued driving him to work from his new place and grew fond of him, too. She was supportive of my marriage to Silvia because she wanted, above all, for me to be happy.

Unfortunately, mom tended to be overly frank and when she got on the phone with Silvia one afternoon she painted such a disconcerting picture of my comings and goings through life that Silvia completely, shall we say, freaked out. Our congeniality dropped to an all-time low and it got to the point where her every utterance became a shrill, lacerating indictment of my chronic irresponsibility. "You're right," I finally assented, exhausted. "I'm a completely worthless jerk, and we should call the whole thing off right now." I hung up.

That was the first time I allowed myself to envision life without her. There are times when the entire fabric of existence is nothing but a Truman Show, and all of reality amounts to no more than random scenes painted on a backdrop behind which workmen scramble to keep the panels from falling onto the stage, to keep the Sun and the Moon from rising and setting at the wrong time or place. Some reach past that through religion or philosophy; for others it's art, maybe science. For me, it was loving Silvia, and I'd just given that up.

I was numb, but OK. I didn't feel guilty, because she'd forced my hand, and she'd made no effort to make amends, so she was probably OK, too. But a month later I was driving to the post office when the phone rang. The caller ID said "Unavailable," so I knew it was international. "Don't you think we should give ourselves another chance?" Silvia asked. "I can't not love you, Silvia, but you just make it impossible sometimes," I sniveled. "I know, I know," she answered. "But it'll be different this time. I've been a fool, Daniel. I love you."

Around that time I was offered a position with the Virginia judiciary. The Supreme Court had started a Foreign Language Services program to oversee court interpreting requirements statewide. The pay wasn't great but in light of Silvia's oft-stated preoccupation over my financial stability, I asked her if she'd rather have an occasionally affluent husband or a dependable provider of modest means. She chose the latter so I took the job, thus becoming an early player in a substantial system overhaul, a role I felt particularly well suited for.

As a civil servant the money was tight, but I had paid holidays, a radically new concept for me. Once there was a five-day Thanksgiving break and I wanted to visit Silvia, but she insisted that we meet in San Andrés, a Colombian resort island off the coast of Nicaragua. After so much time apart, she said, she wanted to have me all to herself; a few days at home in Bogotá just wouldn't do. But I couldn't afford it. "You'd rather not see me at all if we can't go to San Andrés?" I asked her. "No. Just send the money," she answered, meaning my airfare.

Silvia was still keeping our marriage a secret from her ex-husband. I couldn't see why, as she'd assured me that he was a reliable provider to Verónica and Marcela, and that she was not a beneficiary of those arrangements. If so, there was no risk in coming clean with him; if not, however, it seemed to me that she'd be wrong in claiming benefits she might have previously been entitled to. "It's not like that in Colombia," she explained, impatiently. "Alimony doesn't exist here." So why the constant prodding about my ability to support her?

Why should she hide her new status if, as she told me, she was financially independent? When I asked about the girls, their living expenses, college, she had a pat answer: "That's what they have a father for. I've raised them by myself and they're big girls now. Sergio was never around. The least he can do is see them through college." I agreed, but still thought they should prepare to travel also, or at least have their visas ready, because they'd no longer have that option once they turned twenty-one. They could find themselves trapped apart.

She finally agreed to break the news to Sergio, and his response was full-blown denial. Four years after their divorce, he still expected her to be a stay-at-home mom and cater to his daughters' every need until they flew the coop... and maybe even then remain a dutiful, chaste homebody, candle always in the window, so he might return someday, no longer able to sustain his girlfriends' interest, and Silvia would clip his toenails again. It never crossed his mind that she might dare challenge his unilateral interpretation of their divorce arrangements, so he decided it simply wasn't true.

Just in case, however, and to show that he meant business, he withheld tuition for Marcela's college that semester, a mere two weeks before it was due. He knew how to break a woman—he'd learned from the best. Again I had plans to see Silvia, but I spent what I had for that, and then some, to keep Marcela in school when it appeared that no one else was stepping up to bat. Yet Silvia, rather than commend me for such a fine piece of financial brinksmanship, took the "I told you so" route: "I never should have told him, but I had to listen to you."

Bachelors' degrees in Colombia, followed by graduate school in the U.S., or at least transferring their degrees so that they could aspire to better jobs here, were options I had weighed when considering their future. I thought they'd have their father's cooperation, as he surely couldn't fail to see the advantages of bilingual skills and an international background even if they later decided to return. This incredible piece of macho savagery, however, cast all such plans overboard and left us instead with an immediate, excruciating emergency.

Verónica, a flighty, prissy tomboy, had always been daddy's girl and was spared the major's mighty wrath... for the moment. I warned Silvia, however, that it was sure to come, if his state of mind was bent on retaliation, and we'd best start thinking about the girls joining us and maybe working their way through college, as I was unable for the moment to foot the bill, much as I'd like to. Leaving them in Colombia was out of the question now that their father had turned against them, so their problem had become ours, even if we hadn't caused it.

What a tangled web we'd woven—or Silvia had, by so misjudging how our marriage would affect her children's lives. And yet she laid the blame on me, because the problem, in her mind, wasn't that she'd remarried, but that Sergio had found out. It was useless to point out how futile it would have been to drag the secret out forever, not to mention the inherent dishonesty of doing so, and the simple fact that the primary responsibility for determining all of this beforehand was hers, as I clearly lacked the elements to make the call—how could *I* know?

It became one big whatever. I'd already submitted the Petition for Alien Relative, USCIS Form I-30, listing Verónica and Marcela as dependent children traveling with or shortly after their mother. I anticipated they'd be joining us *after* college, but I wanted to make sure their visas were issued before they reached adulthood, which was fast coming up, because they'd lose that right thereafter. All that really changed, then, was that they'd be emigrating sooner than expected. Meanwhile, at least, they were both enrolled for the current semester.

Norma called me unexpectedly from North Carolina one day, announcing that she'd be making a stop in Leesburg on her way to New Jersey, where she'd been staying with a friend who had a Ferrari and a flower shop, she told me, that supplied major hotels and casinos in Atlantic City. Her friend was still on good terms with ex-husband Fred, an elderly gentleman who had set her up in business and was now courting Norma, who, though still married to Héctor, had made a deal with him to snag a *gringo* for visa purposes, divorce him and later reunite.

The blatant, sheer tawdriness of the arrangement made my head spin, but I withheld judgment, not knowing what circumstances they faced in Colombia, where Héctor's livelihood apparently had taken a turn for the worse and they were desperate, about to lose their home. Yet Héctor himself had been unable to stomach the marriage-for-visa scheme when he'd lived for months with me before, and objected strenuously to Norma carrying through with it when her friend set her up with a prospective suitor, the man who had made her rich.

Norma asked me to pick her up at the Washington bus depot, where she was arriving from Raleigh after spending a month with another friend to ward off Fred's advances, claiming that she had changed her mind about the marriage scam. It was actually Héctor who had changed *his* mind, so Norma was trapped in a sticky situation and needed time out. Raleigh, however, turned out even worse, because her friend was rarely home and the husband distinctly disliked her; he went out of his way to make Norma feel unwelcome.

She waited six hours at the station, because I was out of town and wouldn't be back till evening. She was lucky I could pick her up at all, because we'd made no arrangements and it was pure coincidence that I was returning that day. I took her to a Mexican restaurant that makes great flank steak, but she spent the whole time on the phone with Fred, lying to him that she'd been at her brother-in-law's all month. I was uneasy enough to be a part of her cover story, but then she put *me* on the phone to vouch for her. I was fuming, but I played along.

I gave her my bed—the same one her husband had slept in months earlier—and spent the night in Lizzie's room, the kids being at their mom's. Norma was up at six and turned down my offer to make her breakfast because she'd be late for the Atlantic City bus at eight. It wasn't until later that it dawned on me that the entire purpose of her whirlwind Leesburg tour (she didn't even *see* the town by daylight) was to set up her alibi with Fred. She was probably going to show him the ticket "proving" that she'd been in Leesburg all along.

She asked for my advice, and I said it wasn't up to me if she loved her husband or not. What she was really asking, though, was if she should go ahead and have sex with Fred to whet his interest, or would that make a bad impression and instead hurt her chances of marrying him. "Aren't you still married to Héctor?" I asked. "In a manner of speaking, yes," she answered, as if the issue were no more than a technical nuisance. "You can't marry in the United States," I explained, "if you're already married somewhere else." But she was unimpressed.

I was on the phone with Silvia that evening, and mentioned the strange episode. She said that Norma had left Atlantic City because her friend was away for the month and she felt awkward staying alone in her house, that Fred might get the wrong idea. "But isn't her job there?" I asked, puzzled. It turned out later that there had been a falling out between them, over Fred, and Norma no longer worked at the flower shop. She was starting a new job with some connections she had made, and wouldn't be living with her friend anymore.

I left it alone, because Silvia didn't share my opinion that the whole affair showed exceedingly poor judgment, and even worse taste. It was none of my business, anyway, but for the fact that I had been dragged into it as a useful pawn and was ambushed into complicity with Norma's mendacity. As in the case of Silvia's niece, I had only been told what they wanted me to know, or believe, and the fact that none of it made any sense was nobody's problem but my own. So I took the *rolo* way out, and swept the elephant under the rug.

Besides, who was I to question her sister's honesty, when I myself had lied to Silvia about applying for her visa? Earlier, when she had finally supplied me with all the documents to complete the I-30 and made up her mind that she wasn't going to Spain after all,

I didn't have the money for the application fee, which she took to mean that I had never been serious about the marriage and was playing games with her. I could never live it down: "You should have checked your pocketbook before deciding to get married," she taunted almost daily.

I shared my frustration with Orestes, an old friend I'd sometimes have a beer with after work. He laughed at the self-defeating earnestness with which I reported to Silvia every twist and turn of my financial status. "Why does she have to know?" he suggested. "Just tell her that you already did it." I was going to, anyway, as soon as I got the money; I was expecting a check from a recent freelance job so I knew I was covered. Orestes was right: it wouldn't hurt Silvia not to know, and in the meantime I could get her off my back.

But I was a lousy liar. Maybe that was why I was so little fond of lying, not out of an abundance of virtue, but for lack of skill: in less than a week I had already spilled the beans to Silvia about my artless deceit. Once the visa application went through she eased up on the browbeating, but my Big Lie remained a black mark on my character that absolved her from responsibility for anything that ever went wrong between us. She was right: I was a liar, if poorly equipped. Her indictment was the truth, and nothing but the truth, abbreviated.

Cancún

In April an international finance group was holding a conference in Mexico and I was hired as an interpreter. I saw a chance to spend a few days with Silvia on the Caribbean again and asked her to meet me in Cancún. Although by then her U.S. visa was assured, the Mexican embassy was stalling on a tourist visa for this trip, so I talked to a friend at the Pentagon who had diplomatic connections, and they finally granted it the day before her travel date. I was going to see her again, and I was delirious.

I met her at the Cancún airport Friday afternoon. "In all of two years, you couldn't come to see me once?" were the first words out of her mouth. As always, the mere sight of her left me breathless, and I was oblivious to her recrimination—no point in reminding her how and why all of my plans had been frustrated. She's here, I figured, so why waste time on arguments. It was a huge event, and the Mexican government had taken over the town. We got through tight security and she stayed in the room as I left for work. I was interpreting for the President.

He was good; something about building bridges, not walls. My colleague in the booth, a Kennedy-era veteran, waved me on when the standard half-hour shift was up, so I interpreted straight through. There was an endless entertainment program, with a faux-Aztec dance troupe and a battalion-strength mariachi band. It was forty miles from the hotel, at Xcaret, on the "Mayan Riviera" (what a name), and all I could think of was to be with my wife again. Somebody in logistics got me a ride, and I was back in Cancún some time after midnight.

She was sleeping. I sat on the edge of the bed and watched her. She was sucking her thumb in a steady, autonomous rhythm, like a breastfeeding infant. I slipped under the sheets beside her, not touching her, just close enough to sense the smell and warmth of her body. Replacing her thumb with my ring and middle fingers, I marveled at the force with which she sucked them. She was fully relaxed and her vagina yielded freely to the entry of my yearning cock.

"What time did you get back?" she mumbled groggily in the morning. "Late," I said, laconic. A pregnant pause, and then:

"Aren't you going to fuck me?"

"I already did." Wonder flashing in her eyes, she reached between her thighs. "You dirty bastard!" she laughed, wiping her fingers on my chest. "Sorry you missed it," I snickered, turning away. She rose to let the breeze in. The balcony curtains billowed softly as a solid field of cloudless sky and turquoise sea silhouetted her stretching body, lightly covered in a champagne silk dishabille, the first I ever gave her, and still her favorite: a simple, delicate tribute to her bursting physical exuberance, now displayed before me in the golden, Maxfield Parrish morning glow.

When I joined her, the near field came into view, the waters outside the conference center patrolled by Navy fast boats deployed from a destroyer farther asea. We kissed and fondled, wickedly aroused by the inevitable thousand eyes of the heavy surveillance all around us. "They're watching us," she smiled, pulling up the nightie just enough to reveal the parting mounds of her tawny, perfect ass. As they grew in force my thrusts began to lift her up against the railing, twenty-three stories above the lobster-skinned fat tourists feeding at a breakfast trough by the pool.

Silvia's issues yielded to her single-minded pursuit of carnal knowledge. After dinner that evening she said she had "something special" for me. She laid me on my back and took in my penis—*all* of it—locking her lips around it to create a strong vacuum that drew it in, like that first night with my fingers as she slept. I surrendered to her control: planting her vulva firmly against my mouth, she owned me as I exploded in hers, then came around and kissed me deeply, sharing the warm effluence she had collected.

I had some time again the following day so we went into town to try a traditional lime soup someone suggested. It was tepid, and the rest of the meal not much better, but we were in Mexico and I was reluctant to line up with all the *gringos* at the Outback, Olive Garden or other chain eateries along the strip. Silvia, though, was disappointed with the local fare, so I promised not to "go native" anymore. I had meal tickets, anyway, and not a lot of time, so we ate with the delegates, mostly.

Except for Isla Mujeres.

There was a ferry to the island, which was visible a few miles offshore. It was our last day together, and we were running out of time. As we waited at the wharf, I chatted up a red-haired, red-skinned schoolgirl of intriguing ethnic origin and bold proportions. She was flirty, coy, precocious; Silvia smiled. On the boat, two young artists sang and played maracas to Shakira and Celia Cruz soundtracks, then joined us in a bout of lively repartee. I was aware of a sexual force field that drew people to us when we were together—a complicity, like at Guantánamo.

They told us where to find the best fried fish in town. We were hungry, so we went there first. The fish was as good as they said, and the beer as cold as might still be liquid. We walked across the island to the outer shore and leaned against an old stone wall, our senses ravished by the evening breeze. "It comes from Africa," I noted, gesturing vaguely eastward. We kissed endlessly with near-painful, rapt abandon, perfect kisses such as rarely one experiences in a lifetime. On the way back we found an eighteenth-century church where Silvia knelt and prayed as children played in the park outside.

Next morning was a blur. We went shopping for last-minute souvenirs at a nearby mall, and Silvia threw a fit as I was choosing a bead necklace for Lizzie. She disappeared without a word and I spent half an hour looking for her all over the mall. When I found her she acted as if nothing at all was the matter; there was no time for arguments or explanations so I had to let it go, though stinging tears of anger and frustration welled up in my eyes. I boarded my flight an hour after I saw her off to hers. In a couple of months she'd be with me for good.

Leesburg

Back at the courthouse it was business as usual, although I was constantly daydreaming on the job. Between arraignments, detention hearings and bond motions my mind floated away to balconies in heaven and stone walls by the sea, where unbound passion mingled with infantile tantrums and epic sex vied with weird thumb-sucking games on my tableau of earthly delights. We were on the home stretch to becoming a "normal" couple, and my nesting instinct went into overdrive, getting every detail ready for Silvia's arrival. I was on cloud nine.

Then she got a letter from the National Visa Center. Dependent children didn't enjoy "derivative status" on the primary visa application. You get what you pay for, I realized: the immigration lawyer I'd consulted with for free wasn't familiar with certain differences between family visas requested by U.S. citizens, and those requested by resident aliens—green card holders—the cases he usually worked on. Verónica and Marcela had to be applied for separately, but the Visa Center didn't bother to tell us until one month before Silvia's interview date.

"But Silvia, they never said anything," I pleaded. "From the original application, all the way through the screening process, and later when the case was forwarded to the NVC, nobody ever said the girls weren't included, and they were named in the application, clear as day." It had been my idea, in the first place, to even apply for the girls' visas, just to be safe. But Silvia took the position that I was disingenuous, that I had planned this all along, not to burden myself with unwanted responsibilities. "If they don't come, I don't come," she threatened.

She gave me until May the twelfth, our second wedding anniversary, to take care of everything. "What if the twelfth is a Sunday?" I asked, hoping for some flexibility. "If the twelfth is a Sunday, you have until the thirteenth," she yielded. "And if they tell me they can't get it till the fourteenth?" I saw myself as Abraham bargaining for Sodom (I *was* bargaining for Sodom, in a way). "Just do it," she snapped back, like a Nike commercial. I thought I'd already done it, but I hadn't done it right, so I had to do it again.

"OK," I said. "I'll do it."

The embassy gave her an appointment for the ninth. I held out hope that the girls could still be included, because it was an innocent mistake and perhaps the consulate had some leeway. I encouraged them to show up anyway, with all relevant documentation, but they weren't even allowed into the building—adding insult to injury, as Major Morales's daughters weren't used to being turned away from most places. Silvia was approved, and she gave me a reprieve on the girls' visas; at least I'd finally put in the applications, she conceded.

She'd be traveling in style. I got her a window seat on the very first run of Avianca's Flight 286, nonstop from Bogotá to Dulles International, in a brand-new Airbus A-319. They kept her nearly two hours in customs, but being somewhat Colombian I'd come to expect that: the DEA still didn't realize that smuggling cocaine isn't our default setting. She must have fit the profile; she was the last passenger to straggle out, exhausted, as I was readying to storm the gate to find out where she was. International processing areas are about as opaque as the Bermuda Triangle.

During the ride home from the airport, Silvia's first impressions of her new surroundings were unfavorable. The late-spring Virginia foliage was at its lushest, but to her seemed drab, monotonous. The acres upon acres of brand-new homes sprouting like mushrooms all over Loudoun, the fastest-growing county in the nation at the time, seemed artificial, toy-like. Being a harsh critic of local architecture, I had to agree with her on that, but it still beat the squalor of many Bogotá neighborhoods, or our own inner cities, for that matter.

It didn't help her disposition to find the Zapf kids sitting on our doorstep, desperate and forlorn, when we got home. Mark, Anna and Peter were the children of Bruno and Yolanda Zapf, a German couple that had been my neighbors at a previous address, and seemed doomed by Yolanda's consumptive depression to ever-deepening crises. "Where's your mom?" I asked Mark, the oldest. "She went to the gas station to call the police," he replied in a sullen monotone. "Why? What happened?" I asked. "My daddy left us," cried Peter, an exceptionally bright four-year-old.

The police arrived and asked me what was going on, but I had no idea. Yolanda appeared and started rambling about Bruno dumping them at the recreation center where they'd gone swimming. They had walked nearly two miles to my house. Then Bruno showed up, explaining that he had merely returned home for his swimming trunks, that Yolanda had failed to pack. The officer shrugged and left, and I introduced the entire Zapf family to my wife. I hadn't noticed that my friend Orestes had been standing there all along, with a bouquet for Silvia.

The Zapfs left and Orestes came in, but Silvia's bags were still in the car and she was looking dazed, so I asked him to come back later. I showed her upstairs: I had cleared half of the closet, one of the dressers, a nightstand and a long, low table on the window side of the room, for her use. I offered to help, but she asked me to leave her alone. I didn't think it was a good idea but I honored her request, and she came downstairs after a while.

"If this doesn't work out," she said, "you promised you wouldn't hold me to my commitment, right? I mean, we can still be friends..."

"Yes, Silvia, but I was assuming a good faith effort from you to *make* it work."

The sun hadn't set on the first day of our life together, and she was already planning an exit strategy. We were interrupted by a phone call from Lizzie. She needed me to pick her up from a friend's in Purcellville.

"Let's go for a ride," I said to Silvia. "I'd like you to meet my daughter." When we picked her up they exchanged ice-cold glances and monosyllabic grunts of acknowledgment. Returning to Leesburg I chattered desperately against the dead silence in the car.

I didn't ask, but at bedtime Silvia suggested that we hold off on sex until she felt a little less unsettled. That was fine with me, and I even joined her in praying the rosary. The beads used to belong to her mother, who'd died young some ten years earlier; running them through her fingers was a powerful source of comfort for Silvia. She would also read aloud to me in bed, from a Paulo Coelho book about a Brazilian country girl who gets picked up by a Swiss pimp and works as a prostitute in Geneva for a number of years—a charming lullaby.

We got back to our sex frolic, but there was a mildly incestuous flavor to it, seeing now that what I had on my hands was a lost little girl that didn't seem to know what she'd walked into. My demeanor was more fatherly than husbandly as we continued to cultivate our garden of intimate delights, but her apprehensions, doubts and insecurities cast a pall of uncertainty on the viability of the marriage. More often than not our sexual encounters would segue into arguments over money. And then Sergio cut off Verónica's college tuition, too.

No one action can be singled out as the cause of our growing estrangement, but the predicament in which their father left Verónica and Marcela in reprisal for their mother's self-determination of a life goal that conflicted with his plans certainly surpassed, by far, all the other hurdles we encountered in the struggle to be a couple. Now with two college students to worry about, and no idea when their visas would come through, my outlays were extended so far beyond my means that I began to lean on friends and family to make ends meet.

Not that I had never done that before. In fact, the most disturbing part of my mother's candid revelations to Silvia during that fateful phone call that ended our marriage for a month, was precisely my chronic incompetence in money matters. My father had been like that too, but he came from money, so he was able to keep the wolves at bay until he died, still managing to leave his *gringa* widow a respectable pension and a nice house. My grandfather's money was long gone, though, and I had to fend for myself, however ill equipped.

And Sergio, besides, did screw us royally. Though the girls' education wasn't formally my responsibility, and in spite of Silvia's lack of foresight being a key factor in the debacle, I felt obligated, by simple solidarity and perhaps a touch of guilt, to see Verónica and Marcela through these dire straits. All my efforts, however, went unappreciated by Silvia, who even claimed that I already "owed" her the tuition funds I rustled up by hook or by crook, because I hadn't been posting her remittances in the full amount I had "promised" her.

Once each crisis subsided, though, and the immediate contingency was dealt with—

usually, by going further into debt—she'd ease up on the criticism and engage me again in light-hearted conversation as a prelude to sex. We'd drink and smoke sitting on upturned buckets in the back yard. A rabbit always came up and peered at us and we called him Harry. There was still a lot of the wit and whimsy that used to fuel our early midnight chats, and I would often make love to her afterwards thinking that we'd make it, eventually, no matter what.

Fire & Ice

From the day she arrived I strove to include Silvia in all of my social circles and activities. Though I had a cozy position with the state court system, I still took assignments in Washington to supplement my income, and I'd bring her along on occasion to rub elbows with a somewhat worldlier crowd. She liked mingling with people from other countries at international conferences and big diplomatic events where my friends and colleagues would sometimes share with her a favorable opinion of me. I wanted her, by feeling proud of me, to experience a sense of substance.

The interpreter coordinator at DC Superior Court, a man I admired for his adroit manner with all sorts of people and the cool effectiveness with which he ran language services for a complex federal jurisdiction, organized a cookout at his Alexandria home and invited every Colombian interpreter he knew. It was a welcome dinner for Silvia, a memorable event, the sweetest thing Henry ever did for me—and he'd done many. She rose to the occasion and spoke eloquently, after dinner, of her appreciation for such a thoughtful gesture.

On the way back she was aroused and started pawing at my fly as soon as we cleared Henry's driveway. She lunged at my cock while fingering herself with her knees wide apart, propping her feet on the dashboard as she whipped both of our genitalia to a fever pitch. I could barely drive, but was in awe of the strength of her sex drive and didn't want to discourage her ardor on such, for me, auspicious occasions.

"Should we get a room?" I'd kid her, but usually we managed to get home before draining ourselves of such scorching heat.

She was especially fond of Laura, a Mexican friend and colleague in the court system who wanted to show her the ropes of the country she'd adopted by marriage; she'd borne her three children here and built a career by dint of struggle and sacrifice. They also both liked really cold beer, so when I came over to pick Silvia up the extraction could be dicey sometimes. On one such evening Laura, who could become mildly belligerent after a few, had had a few more than a few and decided to argue with me over something that Silvia had said, not I.

I was able to quell the flare-up without incident, and Silvia came along peaceably. She was affectionate en route, and expressed it with tender caresses that covered my eyes as I drove up the Washington Beltway in heavy four-lane traffic at seventy-five miles an hour. I pushed her hand aside briskly, at first with a gentle safety reminder, but then more sternly as she repeated the motion, and I the deflection, again and again. "Are you always suicidal when you get drunk?" I finally exploded, seriously flustered, truly afraid that she was going to get us killed.

She ripped into me. She'd done it before, in a subtly aggressive tone she sporadically adopted when denied something she wanted. But this time it was the full monty: "That's why your first wife left you," she hissed venomously. "You lack what it takes to win the love of a woman. You've wasted your life and take out your frustration on anyone foolish enough to care about you. Your mother never taught you responsibility, so when things go wrong all you know to do is to whine and blame others, like a little girl. You should be wearing a dress."

For being drunk, she was dreadfully eloquent. Relentless, too: that night after Laura's she hurled invective at me for a whole hour. She was eerily comfortable, as if she'd hit her stride. I cowered in fetal position against the headboard of our bed, sobbing helplessly over so dismal a turn of fate. The content of her rant was inconsequential relative to the steady ghoulish outpouring from the deepest recesses of where her soul was supposed to be. Then, as suddenly as it started, it stopped, and she fell asleep. In the morning, she didn't remember a thing.

Another one of her drinking pals was Sandra, a *soi-disant* artist and intellectual who thought that entitled her to marry me. The catastrophic collapse of her three previous marriages, however, argued strongly against such a notion. She panned my lust for "ignorant" women, yet her own frivolous tastes rested on little more than stale formal theory and academic shibboleths. A synthetic dichotomy between "painting" and "illustration" was proof enough, for her, of the irrelevance of representational technique in twentieth-century art—in other words, she couldn't draw.

Yet Sandra befriended the very dumb bunnies she rebuked me for taking as lovers —the better to build her case that I was fucking beneath my station. Silvia, for her part, welcomed the opportunity to gather more dirt on me, so I was a fool to fuel these sessions with generous helpings of salami or prosciutto, crackers, wine and cheese, usually a nice Manchego or Gruyère. The two women quickly went through two bottles of Rioja on one such occasion and, although I wanted to leave, Silvia insisted on staying till Sandra ran out of cheap beer.

Silvia's vehicular antics had become the norm, but it was a short ride from Sandra's so when we got home she was still just warming up. She had me carry her upstairs and I lavished attention on her with most of her clothes still on, bringing her to a respectable triple climax before I rose to wash my hands (I excited her rectally, working her perineal

sponge to give the release extra power).
When I returned she was bare and wide open,
a mischievous grin on her face, pretending to
sleep. I buried my aching flesh deep into the
heat of hers. Suddenly, her eyes came open,
but transfigured, as if possessed—cold and
penetrating, like a knife.

"Do you love me?" she asked.

"Yes, but why are you asking me *now?*"
It was the expression, not the question, that
troubled me.

"If you loved me you wouldn't be doing
this to me," she said.

"What? I don't love you, because I'm
making love to you?"

"You're *raping* me," she spat.

I popped out of her like a papaya seed.
How to understand such a sentiment from
one whose freshly-pleasured naked body lay
sprawled across damp, sultry sheets? Naked,
too, I crouched there, peering, Gollum-like, into
a bottomless pit of nothingness.

"What the hell is wrong with you?"
I demanded, but she'd drifted off into a placid
slumber, which I realized—unfortunately,
much later—was simply a blackout. I hadn't
been on guard for this, but after one alcoholic
marriage I should have recognized the early

warning signs. Desperately trying to rouse her, I brought water from the bathroom in a small mouthwash cup and threw it in her face. She sprang up, sputtering, and I grabbed her by the shoulders.

"Why are you doing this to me? Are you some kind of *freak?*" I cried, thinking somehow I could get through to her. I wasn't aware of the force with which I was holding her, but when I let go she fell back to the bed and reached for her left shoulder. "You hurt me," she said, and for the first time ever I saw fear in her eyes. "So call 911," I blustered. "No goddamn jail can be worse than this hellhole you've dragged us into." And it was true. Our marriage had become Dante's *Commedia,* played out in reverse: *Paradiso, Purgatorio,* and now the *Inferno.*

She didn't call the cops, and I slept in Lizzie's room... or tried to. I was so agitated—panting quick and shallow, my heartbeat pounding in my temples—that I thought of calling 911 myself. The tachycardia subsided and all that remained of my encounter with Beelzebub was the bleak certainty that something had died. I had laid hands on my wife, and she had desecrated our sexual union. Whether she was to blame, or I, or the bottle, it was done. I was already downstairs when she got up around eleven and made us coffee. I didn't say a thing.

Getting By

We were still waiting for the girls' visa interview in Bogotá. I hoped that their arrival, by removing Silvia's most bitter complaint, would level the playing field and give us another shot at love. I studiously avoided any occasion for conflict, although that very evasiveness triggered new remonstrances by her, yet none as brutal as her recent alcoholic tirades. I struggled to persuade myself that those incidents had been momentary imbalances, extreme manifestations of culture shock lashing out, and tried to focus on the future, on building a life together.

Silvia started making lunch daily. I enjoyed coming home, and she felt that she was making a dent in my habitual overspending by not eating out, although she'd sometimes join me downtown and we'd go to the Catoctin Diner or a nearby Chinese restaurant to break up the routine a bit. We had hit a comfortable stride and seemed to have attained a reasonable division of labor.

She was proud of her contribution and I thanked her earnestly, because I appreciated the growing sense of home. Sometimes we'd make love, and I'd be late back to work.

When there were contractors I was particularly fond of in the courthouse, I'd bring them home with me. I'd call Silvia to ask if it was OK, and she'd add little touches to lunch for our guests' enjoyment. I was proud to show her off, and she liked meeting my friends. One of them was Pete Rodríguez, a swarthy Dominican rascal, an incorrigible flirt, a brilliant interpreter and a deeply decent, caring man. He was a huge hit: he praised her cooking to high heaven, and ate with conspicuous relish. "Just like mom's," he said, smacking his chops. Silvia glowed.

But she was restless. Increasingly she'd take to the street, ostensibly to find a job. She felt pressured to work, although I told her we were not actually experiencing hardship but occasional shortfalls, in no small part because of the six- to seven-hundred-dollar phone bills she was running up with her constant, lengthy calls to Colombia. The girls weren't doing well, she said, and she had to check on them. I tried to convince her that spending all that money on phone calls was hurting the girls, not helping them, because it was hurting us—a lot.

She'd promise to cut back, but it was always the same. I was at my wits' end. Couldn't she see that she was driving us deeper and deeper into the red? But she blamed it on me: if I hadn't screwed up the girls' visas (deliberately, she'd often add) we wouldn't have this problem. No matter that our phone plan had free minutes on weekends and after nine on weeknights, which was eight o'clock in Colombia, a perfectly reasonable time to call. And that was just the airtime; international tolls went on call cards that she purchased separately.

I didn't work enough, she insisted. An old Colombian friend had run afoul of the U.S. Office of Foreign Assets Control because of his managerial work with an engineering firm that had been tainted at some point with drug money. He had a clear-cut defense, but getting it through the OFAC bureaucracy was a nightmare. I offered to help him *pro bono*, but the company got involved and the job became a profitable translation project. I had plenty of time in the evenings, Silvia pointed out, and if I really bore down I could bring in good money. But I was tired.

"What if you work for both of us," she suggested, "and I take over the household chores?" We were already doing that, so maybe she just meant that she wasn't going to charge me a hundred dollars per cleaning anymore, a habit she'd gotten into from the first time she picked up a broom. I had tried to explain that she was entitled to my money anyhow, but she insisted on taking it as "payment." She'd *earned* it—no sense of teamwork, partnership. So I said no, on principle. I needed her to accept responsibility for *something*.

To her it meant that I was unwilling to support her, and she went as far as claiming that I had brought her to the States to exploit her, to enslave her. Her claims got more and more outlandish: she'd left everything behind for my sake, abandoned her daughters and turned down job offers just to be with me. What kind of games was I playing? What kind of a husband was I? Even though I'd picked up the tab for Marcela's tuition, when her father cut her off, and also Verónica's, when he did the same to her, everything was still my fault.

Her critical vitriol soared to messianic heights. Despite her own towering self-importance, she saw herself as a spokesperson for an even higher power, as an agent of God's wrath, an executor of His will. She berated me for things that I was proud of, that represented some degree of achievement or satisfaction, for no other reason than to spite me. If I enjoyed someone's friendship or expressed admiration for another person, she'd hasten to tear them down, digging up imperfections that diminished them in her eyes, and therefore God's.

In my moments of weakness and vulnerability, she would remind me that I had brought my misfortunes upon myself, particularly regarding her disaffection. She'd lecture that I had undervalued her greatness as a woman, and had thrown away God's greatest gift to me, which was she. When I most needed understanding and compassion from a loving partner, she would demonstrate quite pointedly, and ruthlessly, that I was alone. Good thing I didn't believe her, because I would've had to shoot myself—so slight, in her eyes, was my value as a man.

Jerry Parker, a friend who had lived in Colombia for a few years, invited us to the beach in late summer. Silvia took the front seat of his BMW and pumped his ego with flattery and coy flirtation, creating a tense, competitive atmosphere reminiscent of Polanski's *Knife in the Water.* Atypically cocky, Jerry bet me a hundred dollars that Beethoven's *Hammerklavier* sonata, playing on the radio, was Opus 111 and not, as I knew, 106. He never paid me; it was all about impressing Silvia. She was poisoning my relationships with friends.

Her absences became more frequent and extended, and we rarely had lunch together anymore. She was looking for a job, she told me. One evening around eight she burst into the house crying bitterly. She'd been cleaning houses all day and was paid a paltry forty-five dollars. She'd never been so humiliated in her life. "But why did you do it?" I asked. "Because you force me to; we're always broke, and I don't know English so I can't work in my field."

I took her much-vaunted professional status with a grain of salt. She had completed a few semesters in the social work school of an obscure university in northern Colombia. At the time I encouraged her to parlay her experience into a professional career in the States, and hinted that college degrees aren't so hard to come by in Colombia. It didn't take much coaxing: soon she was proudly brandishing a diploma from that university, which cost me another couple million pesos. She assured me she had taken all the exams, and it was legit.

Knowing how strongly she felt about working out regularly, I had enrolled her in a local gym and dropped her off on my way to work. It wasn't far from the house, so sometimes she would walk there later in the morning, and I'd pick her up during my lunch break. She'd be waiting outside, sweatshirt sleeves tied around her waist, the rest of the garment covering her behind—to keep men from looking, she said; but then why make such a big deal of shaping and firming it? I thought instead it was some kind of silly *rola* fashion statement.

She landed a job at the Thai Garden, a restaurant whose owner she met at the gym. They'd struck up a conversation and Silvia mentioned she was looking for work. Her English was "no good"—meaning *not* good— but Jasmine told her she could bus tables and bring out meals. The job was beneath her, she felt, but it was easy and they were nice. She had a big grin on her face when she came home with her first paycheck. It was just a temporary fix, I reminded her; with English and some academic work she'd probably soon be making more than I was.

But she had a fundamental inability to grasp the oh-so-American notion of the working couple. The more I insisted on the importance of a woman's financial independence from a man, plus the additional perk of a higher combined income, the more she felt I was shirking some primal obligation to "take care" of her. Rather than a step to freedom, a chance to love a man for the man himself, while building a better life together, in her eyes what I suggested was enslavement, exploitation, and she was vehement that her money be exclusively hers.

Which was fine with me, if it made her more comfortable as she got the hang of things—she wasn't making that much, anyway, at twelve to sixteen hours a week, so it was a chance to prove to her that *Arbeit macht frei*. To further liberate her from the kind of husband worship that had made her so miserable for twenty years, I enrolled her in English classes at the local community college. There were two sections, each two evenings a week, covering conversation and grammar, respectively. I dropped her off and picked her up nightly.

But she was tortured by angst over her daughters. Since they were "all grown up" she had left them in their Bogotá apartment to fend for themselves, but at last report they were eating popcorn and potato chips, and Marcela would lock herself in her room and refuse to talk to anyone. Silvia's sisters nagged her constantly: she had abandoned the girls, they said, and if anything untoward were to befall them it would be her fault. I told her they should be able to hold up until their visas came through, but she insisted on going to see them.

There had been complications with her green card, which USCIS had mailed, they said, shortly after her arrival. In the parallel universe of Homeland Security, the fact that it hadn't been returned by the post office meant that they couldn't just issue a new one, and we had to apply—and pay the fee—all over again. Had it *been* returned, of course, it wouldn't in fact be lost, and we wouldn't need a new one. I just didn't get it, somehow. The fact remained that if she left the U.S. without it, there was a pretty good chance she wouldn't be able to reenter.

She didn't care. The girls *needed* her, and she wouldn't be deterred from seeing them by some minutia like the visa she had married for and we'd struggled to secure for years. She seemed to think that just being by their side was going to fix everything, and the problems caused by our marriage would simply go away, their lives then returning to some golden *status quo ante*—infinite variations of the absurd. Norma was in Miami at her best friend Elvira's, and urged Silvia to join her there for the trip to Bogotá together. She already had her ticket.

I got her a ticket to Miami, but the night before the flight she started complaining of extreme abdominal pain. She was clearly going into shock so I rushed her to the hospital against her will; all she could think of was getting on that plane. They gave her morphine and came back with a definitive diagnosis of bile duct obstruction. The nurse, a sweet, very large Trinidadian who had worked for several years in a plastic surgery clinic, revealed to me that the scar that Silvia had always attributed to her C-sections was in fact from a tummy tuck.

"She looks like an angel," said the nurse, referring not to the scar but to the cherubic expression on Silvia's face as she drifted into a narcotic slumber. She did look like a baby, and soon enough she was sucking her thumb. I recalled early chats in which she'd bragged about how flat her tummy was, from working out at the gym, and how her sisters refused to believe her when she insisted that her remarkably perky tush was sculpted by hard exercise, not plastic surgery. "Things that make you go *hmmm,*" I remembered an old song.

The colic subsided but the ER physician insisted that she schedule surgery the very next day, and by no stretch of the imagination should she travel—an in-flight rupture could be fatal, he warned. I took her home and carried her upstairs, much like the evening of her "transfiguration," and waited for the clock to tick past flight time. The serendipity of her illness was beyond belief: maybe now we could work out something reasonable. I'd take her to the doctor first thing in the morning. But suddenly she sprang up, as if struck by lightning.

"What time is it?" she demanded. "Silvia, you can't fly today—doctor's orders." But she was leaving, and that was that. "If you get another attack during the flight, your gallbladder could rupture before the plane can land," I repeated the doctor's warning. It was just a short flight, she countered, and that wasn't going to happen; it was a possibility, not a certainty. Striking, how comfortable she'd suddenly become with uncertainty.

"Well, yes," I granted, "a risk. But a serious one. What good will you be to your daughters if you're dead?"

I was wasting my breath. She started hauling her bags down to the car herself, but I took them from her and carried them instead. I'd had the same condition three years earlier and knew the lingering tenderness. I forgot the tank was empty as we launched into a cannonball run to the airport, a mere fifty minutes before flight time, arguing about her visa, about her illness, about how totally crazy this whole thing was. But she was driven, her mind completely shut to anything I said. And then we ran out of gas, coasting limply off a ramp two exits before the airport.

I snapped. I howled in despair as I slammed my open hands repeatedly against the steering wheel. I burst out of the car and paced back and forth along the gravel shoulder, holding my head with both hands as if it were going to fly off.

"OK," she said, meekly. "I won't go."

I was beside myself, as must be obvious: "Well of course you won't go! Boarding probably already started about ten minutes ago. They may have shut the airplane door already. And here we are, stranded on the highway, as if you ever had a chance of making that flight!

"You know what?" I continued, "If I *had* stopped for gas, that would have eaten up the three or four minutes that we *might* have had to make it, running like idiots through the airport, even if the lines were short going through security." Out of the blue, a comforting thought: I was better off where we were, than getting arrested for an irate confrontation with Homeland Security drones. I did cool off, eventually, and asked Orestes to bring us gas. I still had the card from the hospital—never did change clothes—so I also called to make an appointment with a surgeon.

Once home, I asked her to rest, though I probably needed it more myself. I told her that everything would work out, that she'd go to her daughters, but first she had to have her gallbladder removed. Maybe in the meantime her green card would come in, and she could travel without that extra worry. It wasn't nine yet, so I showered and went to work, not so much out of employee conscientiousness as an overwhelming need to extract myself from the complete insanity that I'd been engulfed in for nearly twenty-four hours. Or maybe longer... far longer.

Greyhound Odyssey

When I returned in the afternoon her bags were by the door again. "I'm taking the bus," she announced. "What about your medical appointment tomorrow?" I objected. But she'd been on the phone with Norma and they'd made arrangements. There was a Greyhound leaving Washington at nine, and would I please drive her to the station. It was supposed to pull into Miami at three the following afternoon, but it seemed to me that buses take longer than that. "It's an express bus," she said her sister had told her. I was too exhausted to fight it, so I said OK.

We had a quick chat on the sidewalk, her bags already in the car. She promised not to leave without a travel permit, which we'd secure in Miami during the two days until her flight. She had painkillers from the hospital, and I made sure she took her phone charger, so we'd be in touch during the bus ride.

"When it's running low and there's a rest stop, plug it in and call me, tell me where you are," I urged her. It turned out to be a wise precaution, because she was on the road for thirty hours—actual arrival time was three *in the morning,* one day later.

There was a sweet tenderness to our many conversations all night and the following day, as she called me nearly hourly to report on her whereabouts and comment on life in general as she saw it since coming to the States. It became abundantly clear that Norma's ETA was off when Silvia made it into Atlanta around noon.

"So I'm three hours from Miami?" she asked, with fetching naïveté. "No way, Silvia. Atlanta's barely halfway there, by a different route. Your sister must have misunderstood whatever information they gave her."

I lived that bus ride as if I were on it. Silvia kept me awake for two consecutive nights, sharing with me her impressions of the people and places she saw from her Greyhound window. With each redeye stop at towns and villages I'd never heard of and she couldn't pronounce anyway, I relived my own reacquaintance with the land of my birth when I came back after growing up in Colombia, and felt again that strange fascination. I also realized how much of our relationship had always been on the phone; it felt comfortable to be back.

When we'd met in Cancún, in fact, I joked with her on our way from the airport (though she was still copping a huff), that I'd gotten us rooms on separate floors so that we could have phone sex at night, and meet for breakfast in the morning. I finally got her to smile—to laugh, actually—and our second honeymoon started looking much better. Now I was her travel log and *tabula rasa*, upon which she scribbled the meanderings of her consciousness as she sorted through the jumbled experiences of an incomprehensible new life in a strange, alien world.

Silvia was brave, if foolhardy, and I admired, oddly enough, her staunch resolve in going through with this harebrained odyssey. It struck me that her decision to marry me was a similar stab in the dark, although her resolve in that case was presently coming undone. Her courage was not matched by her consistency, and her goals would shift with the changing wind. I was an idle bystander as her fate played out erratically, and could aspire to no more than a supporting role, picking up the shattered pieces of anything that stood in her way.

Norma and Elvira picked her up at the depot, hungry and exhausted after eating no more than Cheetos and a sandwich that she could hardly stomach, someplace in Georgia, and barely sleeping for two nights running. I could imagine her dazed excitement at the sight of familiar faces. Her gallbladder had held up, sparing us all an excruciating, dramatic episode in some lost village with an Indian name in the swamps of Georgia or South Carolina; her pointless pilgrimage, amazingly, would go on. In other words, she got away with it.

Norma called me the next morning and subjected me to a machine gun tirade about what Silvia really needed, that I as a husband wasn't giving her. In Colombia she'd have the loving, nurturing support of her family when she went in for surgery, Norma ranted, impervious to the fact that they'd planned the trip *before* she got sick. If I really loved her sister, instead of forcing her to stay with me I should let her go—which, oddly, was what I had just done. I congratulated her for her mindless monologue (she'd rehearsed it for days, probably) and asked to speak to Silvia.

"Well, if your gallbladder ruptures in flight, at least you'll die in your sister's loving arms," I almost said, but we talked instead about her travel permit, a special exemption they'd stamp on her passport at the Miami USCIS office. When she got there they told her that she had to do that in Virginia, her state of residence. But with a little pouting on her part and frantic legwork on mine to fax them certain documents by noon, the permit was finally issued by a nice Cuban man who gave her his phone number and asked her out for dinner.

She pronounced it a miracle, proof that God wanted her to make the trip. She'd said the same thing two days earlier when we'd run out of gas: that was a sign from God to stay home—until Norma called and countermanded Him. The two Cordero sisters took the next flight to Bogotá and Silvia was soon admitted to the *Hospital Militar,* the best in the country, that she still had access to, she said, by virtue of her *former* marriage to a CNP officer, which I thought was strange. She underwent laparoscopic cholecystectomy without incident, and without a single family member present—not even Norma.

I didn't want to admit it, but I felt much better while Silvia was away. We kept in touch on the phone, though not quite as regularly as when we were courting, and she added a new layer of reticence to her return plans. Though I didn't ask, on several occasions she mentioned that she was weighing certain options; but the only point that really came across was that I wasn't the only game in town, or so she wanted me to think. This time, however, I encouraged her to pursue her career goals even if they conflicted with our plans. "Take your time," I told her.

Talking on the phone again restored our intercourse to the mellow, teasing tone of earlier days, and before long we were having phone sex as before, though somewhat tempered by real experience. That she took Simón with her, even though she'd packed her bags in the heat of a medical emergency, was ample proof of an abiding fascination with sex—an addiction, maybe—to match my own lascivious inclination; it was a necessary counterpart to my intemperance, the fifty-one percent of the relationship that was needed for the rest to work.

She mentioned that she'd run into Víctor. He was singing at a restaurant where Gloria had taken her for dinner. "He sings?" I asked. Yes, she said—he was a trained tenor; he would sing along to *Don Giovanni* when they cohabited in Bogotá. So *that's* where she got her Mozart! He called her another day and propositioned her for an affair. She'd turned him down flat, she bragged, as if she'd done me a big favor. But why did he have her number? And what was he doing in Bogotá? Again, she was dissembling, obviously, making two events out of one: she probably had arranged to meet him.

She was away for a couple of months, and it appeared that the pause for reflection had done her some good. Upon returning her attitude was more constructive and her expectations more realistic. She adopted a more thoughtful approach in her job search, capitalizing on her work with the foundation where she'd been involved in adoption and foster care placement of children of unfit mothers. Sandra helped her register with an online roster of childcare providers, and I put together a fairly impressive résumé highlighting her qualifications.

She was open to a broader range of options, not necessarily at the professional level to which she ultimately aspired but for which she fell far short of meeting American language and academic standards... for the time being, I reminded her. The county school system had positions in which English was not an essential requirement, and the human resources representative we talked to was optimistic about her chances as a teacher assistant. Eventually she started getting calls from the nanny list and before long she had several clients.

One of these was a family with a troubled three-year-old that Silvia took up as a personal challenge. She saw that the problem was the parents, an architect-nurse couple struggling with the estrangement caused by the husband's infidelity. She shielded Nathan from their strife and developed a strong bond with him by reading from children's books that also helped her with her English. She strengthened his creative development through art projects that he proudly showed his parents, whose marriage, remarkably, began to mend.

I marveled at her intuitive sensitivity and the effect that she was having on the entire family, which she attributed to her training as a social worker and her practical experience with dysfunctional homes. She'd recount the day's activities and explain her strategies to me when I picked her up from work; I supported her projects with art supplies that she never charged the family for. On my lunch breaks I'd sometimes drop her off a sandwich, and Nathan, who never talked to anyone, would wave at me from the window.

More than a job, Silvia's relationship with Nathan and his parents was a connection to the loving humanity in her that somehow she couldn't extend to me. She herself appreciated the irony and compared it to clinical psychologists who can guide their patients effectively through therapy, yet can themselves sometimes be crippled by problems even worse. The intelligence of those conversations, her cogent, keen reasoning, baffled me all the more at how refractory and irrational she was in dealing with our relationship issues.

I never lost from sight the heady rush of nightly banter, spiced by sex, or vice versa, that had made my relationship with Silvia, beginning with our early friendship, such a constant in my every waking moment, and my dreams. But the trust that had enabled that, a sense of primal innocence in the midst of our glad debauchery, never quite came back from the abysmal depths it had plunged to when resentment and fear—I thought—drove her to lash out at me so relentlessly during our worst times. She had become for me, since then, a different person.

As much as I tried to rationalize her behavior, the pain that her scorn and derision had caused me was more like a physical scar that my conscious efforts could do nothing to suppress. And as much as she tried to control it, the slightest adversity would bring out again the despotic aggressiveness that made her blind to all shades of gray and unyielding in her harsh judgment of matters of which she knew absolutely nothing. She dismissed every argument with which I attempted to address her many misconceptions as mere pretext, subterfuge.

Basically, she didn't trust me. I didn't take that part too personally, though, because I'd already seen, from the way she treated taxi drivers in Bogotá, that she didn't trust anybody. When she arrived in Leesburg she couldn't find a bottle of her favorite perfume, and instantly assumed that Adriana, who helped her pack for the trip, had kept it. But her daughters found it later; she had left it in her dresser. "So your best friend isn't a thief, after all," I prodded. Her distrust was organic; the problem was the mean, offensive way she had of acting it out.

It didn't take a degree in psychology to see that twenty years of lewd effrontery by her first husband had fundamentally damaged her ability to trust other people, and without that, of course, her capacity for love was also seriously impaired. As a knight in shining armor coming to her rescue, I lacked the skills to address such deep-seated systemic issues, and became instead the whipping boy of convenience every time she felt badly about anything at all. Even she could see that, in fleeting moments of insight, but she simply couldn't help it.

Snakes

I was walking down a dusty road one blustery afternoon when I saw a small snake emerging from the bushes, crawling toward the other side. Concerned that a car might run it over, I resolved to remove it to a safer place. Up the hill behind me was the home of a woman my children and I called the Bird Lady, because a veterinarian had sent us to her when we brought him a baby blue jay that had fallen from its nest. She also nurtured other orphaned fauna—rabbits, squirrels—until they could be released back to the wild, so I reckoned she'd welcome the little snake.

From childhood, growing up in Florida, where snakes and other reptiles were common, I'd learned to scoff at the unfounded revulsion most people feel for them, and made much of my ability to distinguish between dangerous and harmless species. My college roommate once found a beautiful tree snake near campus, brought it to the boarding house where we shared quarters, and we named it Clorofila, arbitrarily assuming it was a female due to her slinky, flowing grace and lush green color. We kept her in an aquarium and fed her crickets.

"Clorofila escaped!" we'd shout when she got out of the aquarium, and the boarders would jump on their beds as we looked for her. Her favorite trick was to stretch out along the leaves of a small palm tree in the patio, becoming nearly invisible, but we'd always find her. One day she disappeared for good, just like the iguana I used to keep in our back yard back home in Tuluá. My mother hated it, not out of some primal fear, but because it kept coming into the living room and tore the curtains as it climbed them. I always suspected she'd secretly gotten rid of it.

My children enjoyed these stories immensely and had me tell them over and over as I put them to bed after their mother left us. But I realized I had gone too far when Chris caught a snake by the creek one day and showed it to me proudly when I arrived from work. As I neared my hand it reared its head aggressively and struck the sides of the plastic container in which Chris kept it. We took it to the rescue squad to see if they could identify it, and one of the paramedics told us it was a copperhead. "Your son could have died," he reprimanded me sternly.

When I tried to pick it up, the dusty little snake by the road was just as fierce as Chris's copperhead, but there was more: it spread *a hood!* What on earth was a cobra doing in Virginia? All the more reason to deliver it to safety, as it surely wouldn't survive the winter. Distracting it with a stick while I grabbed it behind the head with my other hand, I put it in the side pocket of a thick canvas jacket I was wearing, knowing that cobras, unlike rattlesnakes, don't have long, hinged fangs. I closed the zipper and turned back up the hill to the Bird Lady's house.

The cobra started slithering out of my pocket, and when I tucked it back in it glanced my hand but didn't quite bite me. Alert to any throbbing or searing sensation, I hastened to the Bird Lady's doorway but the snake got out of my pocket again and sank its teeth in me firmly this time. "Now I'm done for," I thought, and woke up in a cold sweat. Silvia was asleep beside me and I thought to tell her about the nightmare, but her sweet scent and soft warm body soothed me as I cupped her left breast (the smaller one, my favorite) in my snakebit hand and dozed off again.

"Watch out for Evelyn," she told me later, interpreting the dream as a sign that a disloyal coworker was out to get me. During a brief assignment at an earlier jurisdiction, before I assumed my post in Leesburg, I'd caught Evelyn cheating to make her performance seem better than mine, by a margin that made me look like a complete slacker. There were other instances of treachery and deceit that could have cost her her job had I reported her and the director believed me—or me mine if he didn't, so I left it at that, although Silvia insisted that I should go after her: crush the snake's head.

Silvia had an ectoplasmic connection and could sense the presence of spiritual bodies. Looking out the window of an apartment where she'd taken her daughters to a birthday party once, she saw a little girl arrive with her mother in a taxicab, and another girl, about the same age as the first, emerged with them. Silvia asked about this girl, who never came into the apartment, and described her; the mother said she was her daughter's dead twin sister, only visible to certain people. But Silvia had my snake dream wrong: Evelyn was just a worm. Besides, I no longer worked with her. The snake had to be someone else.

Small World

My involvement with the Foreign Language Services division began to branch out into areas I increasingly defined for myself. I wanted to cover languages other than Spanish—LOTS, as the segment is known in court interpreting lingo—and pointed out to Richmond that if we focused exclusively on Spanish we might as well call ourselves SLS instead of FLS. I got permission to launch a LOTS program in my district, emulating the simplicity and effectiveness of what Henry was doing in DC Superior. I called it "Henrification."

For a quarter of a century as a free-lance translator and interpreter I had never had any part in corporate or bureaucratic structures nor had ever had to answer to a "boss," so my newfound ability to fit in with a stolid government organization, aside from surprising me, put to rest my fears that I would always be some sort of Hessian *Steppenwolf,* stalking society from a safe distance. A lawyer that I knew had cautioned that the insertion would stultify me, that it would be "ruinous to your soul, man," but, on the contrary, it revealed to me a hidden capability that pleased me.

Thus a job that I'd initially accepted mostly in response to Silvia's livelihood concerns evolved into a rewarding area of personal endeavor and creative engagement. My pilot program failed to take hold in other jurisdictions, but I drew satisfaction from transforming mine into a "one-stop-shopping" venue. The daily grind was also much relieved by the presence of interpreters from all over the world, whom I added to a growing roster and in some cases became personal friends. I was carving out a niche in the system.

I found a Lebanese interpreter for an Arabic case and we hit it off instantly. Bashir was a Shakespeare scholar with a PhD from Cambridge and could recite at will from the Sonnets. I had a few of my own, one of which I shared with him. "Well, it's not Shakespeare," he chuckled, but encouraged me with thoughtful comment on the poem, an effort to adapt Italian *terza rima* to the outer shape of the Elizabethan sonnet, substituting four daisy-chained tercets for the standard three quatrains, but keeping the final couplet. The hybrid form amused him.

Bashir had been a member of his country's delegation to the United Nations, where he met an American diplomat that he married and stayed to live with in the U.S. His natural business acumen leveraged a small initial investment into a real estate company with properties in Europe, Latin America and the Middle East. I asked him why he bothered with interpreting. "How else would I have ever met you, Daniel?" he laughed. His daughter Nayla was the same age as Lizzie; both were very smart, starting college, and we agreed that they should meet.

Silvia and I were guests at his birthday party a few months later and first experienced there the splendid grace of Arab hospitality. Bashir was the reigning patriarch of a large extended family spanning four generations, and we were treated as if they'd known us forever. We smoked hookah and feasted on savory strips of grilled chicken, fish and beef. Grandparents and children of all ages danced spontaneously to spirited selections of Lebanese and other Arab music that we, too, danced to with rapt abandon. It was just like a Colombian family gathering.

A Fon interpreter from Benin, also moonlighting in my courthouse from his regular embassy job, invited us to his son's wedding when he learned of my fondness for African music, especially from Mali, Senegal and Côte d'Ivoire. Christophe was recently divorced from a regal, sensual goddess of Ghanaian-Togolese extraction, also there, and looked wistfully from the head table as we tried to render the rich, polyrhythmic tunes on the dance floor. He glowed with delight and showed himself an expert when Silvia asked him out to dance.

Moments such as these always revived my belief that Silvia and I had much more in common, all values properly weighted, than any surface noise that came to shroud our underlying consonance. This fundamental attraction, I thought, was stronger than any dissonance that could cleave us, and as long as I believed that, nothing could persuade me to give her up. When this was reinforced by the paroxysm of physical surrender that invariably followed, all lingering discrepancies were washed away by oceanic waves of existential fullness.

"Dance with me," she'd say, and smile.

Additionally, little rituals began to emerge in our daily routine that seemed to validate, in the small, what my instincts told me about the big picture. Usually, they were Silvia's idea. In the morning, for instance, if she was in the shower first, it was my turn to make the bed. Of course she was always first, because she was quick on the draw and always beat me to it, laughing. It was fun racing her to get the bed done, because she also showered very briskly, with near-military discipline, while I was more of a lingerer, but decreasingly so.

Occasionally the lines were blurred and we'd make the bed together, each drawing and plumping our respective side.

I welcomed this quick and neat approach to what I'd always seen as an odious task, dismissing it for years under the bachelor-pad lifestyle that regrettably my kids had also learned. After Silvia, the better practice prevailed and I could no longer stand the sight of unmade beds. I forced the children to make theirs, too, and they grumbled, but usually complied. The dishes, though, were another story altogether, a can of worms.

I was used to doing the dishes, pots and pans every time I prepared food, because I obsessed over having clear counter space for my recipes, which usually involved a lot of slicing and dicing. When Silvia cooked, I'd spontaneously rise to do the dishes, but a macho stereotype in her mind made it unsightly for a man to busy himself with kitchen chores. If Chris or Lizzie left things in the sink, though, she wouldn't touch them, because she was "nobody's maid," she bristled —yet she would also be furious if I simply washed them myself.

While I respected what part of her opinions I saw as constructive criticism of my inadequate parenting skills in some areas— both of us having brought up two children as, mostly, single parents—I objected to the self-righteous way in which she enforced them, especially as I noticed certain excesses in her own standards, like when she made Verónica fail a subject one semester by refusing her cab money to make it on time to the exam, after studying for it all night. "That'll teach her to get up on time," she huffed.

Miami

As Christmas neared Silvia's thoughts turned to Colombia, but another trip so soon after her last one was out of the question. Norma's best friend Elvira, whose home both sisters stayed at when Silvia took the bus there, gave her the next best option by inviting us to Miami for the New Year. We drove all night and Silvia was pleased that I gave her the wheel. She was fine through the Carolinas, but as traffic got heavier her inexperience became apparent and I took over again. We had breakfast in a cracker town east of Gainesville, where my dad had met my mother and I was born.

The sandy white, palmetto-tufted plains brought back my childhood in the Orlando area, long before Disney World. I remembered my first day of school and my mother walking me to the bus stop on a lonely stretch of highway with orange groves on both sides. I was nervous and she taught me to pick up pebbles and throw them out to the field. She used to do that to feel better when she was a girl, she told me, among other stories like catching swimming snakes from a footbridge over a crystal-clear, babbling brook. It all seemed so magical at that age.

We pulled into Miami around four. Elvira lived just off the beach in a second-floor apartment with her boyfriend Tony, an Italian bartender who knew everything. Silvia had a theory about their relationship, revolving around Elvira's immigration status. There could be some of that, I agreed, but what's so wrong, I asked obliquely, about a woman seeking security in a relationship? I sensed no guile or affectation in Elvira's sweet, affectionate manner with her boyfriend; it was more likely that he was using her than the other way around.

It was New Year's Eve and we were expected at the home of Tony's father, who was fond of Elvira and told her to bring us along. Tony's insistence on having his way led to a lovers' quarrel that made us late leaving Elvira's and was still raging when we arrived at Mr. Mancini's, a retired New Jersey police sergeant. He hid the pain that still wracked him from his wife's death, a year earlier, with a crusty, dark, ruthless humor, and regaled us with various Italian delicacies that gathered unto themselves about half the cholesterol in Dade County.

His daughter, Tony's sister Angela, an anchorwoman for a local news channel, was a voluptuous Mediterranean sexpot à la Gina Lollobrigida, married to a petulant Persian businessman who treated her with contempt and kept getting up from the table to take calls on his BlackBerry. Her unhappiness screamed to high heaven, and I would have gladly come to her rescue had I not myself been looking for love in all the wrong places. She was quick with words and sparred with me in lively table talk that made her husband increasingly uncomfortable.

Tony and Elvira had taken their spat to another room and we started without them, our dinner punctuated by occasional choleric outbursts by Mr. Mancini in choice, pungent Hobokenese. Twice he began to leave the table, fully intending to drag Tony back by the ear, but Angela, who had assumed her mother's job of checking her father's quick temper, scolded him like a child and reminded him that there were guests. Changing the subject, he would then flirt with Silvia, and I was forced to interpret for him. Angela couldn't hide her amusement.

She was wearing a khaki shirt dress that struggled to remain buttoned, her buoyant cleavage cleverly revealed, from certain angles, down to the twin lacy edges of a plunge bra that supported her breasts not so much as kept them from flying away to heaven, where they belonged. She rose to play something a little livelier than her father's Italian crooners on the stereo, and I marveled at the impossible flare from her petite waistline to the ample hips and buttocks that she swayed subtly to the music on her way back to the table, smiling serenely.

I could see where her husband's bile came from, though by no means sympathized with him; I myself was close to suffering a hernia both from the (futile) struggle of hiding from Silvia my lascivious interest in Angela, and from the unbearable pressure of a monster erection burgeoning under my zipper. I had half a mind to make a quick trip to the bathroom and be done with it, but just then Tony and Elvira emerged from their two-hour council, holding hands and smiling like idiots. "It's about time," guffawed Mr. Mancini. "It's 2010 already."

I hadn't slept in two days but for a couple of quick naps and was exhausted; our host was drunk, and Angela's husband was making faces at her to leave. As he scowled, she invited us to come and stay sometime at a little hideaway she had in Key West. "It's really nice. I stay there a lot," added Tony, who was in the habit of living off his sister, rent-free. Mr. Mancini wouldn't let go of my hand. "You're alll rright, Danny. You like my yokes." I didn't; they were crude and bigoted. He waved unsteadily from the door as we backed out the driveway and hit the road.

"Did you like her?" Silvia asked me back at the apartment. "Who?" I asked—stupidly, as if she could mean anyone else. I was still in a daze. "You couldn't take your eyes off her," she pressed, and I confessed: "Well, maybe a glance or two... But you have to admit, she's a bombshell." Silvia enjoyed torturing me. "Would you fuck her?" she asked, point-blank. "Are you crazy?" I protested. "That's what I have *you* for! My eyes may wander, but my dick knows its place." She accepted that, and fucked me playfully. As I came, I thought of Angela.

Silvia had amazing shoulders. I had a distaste for round, droopy shoulders, but then most people probably agree that those are less pleasing to the eye, at least by contemporary standards. In my case, though, an early experience with a girl that looked like a hot dog (her slightly acidic body odor, in fact, reminded me of sauerkraut) more or less marked me for life. Silvia rarely slept naked but the Miami subtropical weather, after the snowbound drear we came from, moved her to wanton abandon, her cinnamon flesh sprawled out on the rumpled white sheets, her sharp, straight shoulders at random angles.

I'd been watching her for several minutes, taking in the expressive complexity of her body, when the phone rang. I had told my sister Tracy that we'd be in town a couple of days, and she wanted to take us out. She lived in Miami with her husband Alan, a Belgian Jew who'd made her happy again following years of emptiness after her divorce from her first love, a charming but dissolute man she'd married in Colombia at age seventeen. Elvira had plans for the day—

Friday, January the first—so we'd spend Saturday the second with Tracy.

Elvira asked her in when she arrived to pick us up around noon, and treated us to a hearty Bogotá brunch of *chorizo,* hot cocoa and *arepa,* a grilled cornmeal flatbread with a chewy texture that's delightful with butter or fresh farmer's cheese. Our dad used to make fun of Tracy's air of cosmopolitan refinement—he said she'd learned it from *Cosmopolitan* magazine—but she truly was the family diplomat, and rewarded Elvira's hospitality with lavish compliment of our simple, spot-on repast and an invitation to join us later, for dinner.

Tracy—the youngest of my three sisters, the only one born in Colombia—had become a staunch Miamian since moving there with her first husband in the eighties. This was her home, where she'd raised her children, and she was proud to show us around: Bayside, Little Havana, South Beach, Coconut Grove. We had cappuccinos at a chic coffee shop near the Brickell Avenue high-rise where she and Alan had a condo. We waited there for him to return from walking Mindy, a bichon frise that neither barked nor shed hair: the perfect apartment dweller.

The condo was a minimalist love nest, richly appointed in chartreuse Italian leather, mirror-smooth white marble floors and a Danish stainless steel kitchen. Floor-to-ceiling glass separated both the single bedroom and the living room from a connecting balcony that ran clear across the entire apartment, with a breathtaking 43rd floor view of Biscayne Bay. I pointed out that there was nowhere for guests to stay. Tracy smiled slyly: precisely. Alan walked in with Mindy, who started jumping all over us.

"She's *loca* today," he cautioned, and strode casually across the room to welcome us, wearing long, baggy gym shorts, a perfectly clashing Hawaiian shirt and throwaway flip-flops. His accent, as eclectic as his attire, was completely impossible to place. Alan was a wandering Jew, a world gypsy. He'd been to countless countries and had lived in about six, learning each language in a perfunctory way, speaking not one of them with full fluency— except Yiddish, that he used with his mother, a Holocaust survivor. In a flash, he showered and changed into an identical outfit. "Ready for dinner?" he grinned, boyishly.

"Let's take the big one," he said, when Tracy asked which of the Audis from their color-matched his-and-hers pair to drive to the restaurant. "We'll have people to drop off later," he explained. It struck me, though I'd just met him, that he did things as soon as he thought them, and was usually right. He wasn't at all impulsive; just quick-minded and determined. Tracy told us that he'd set his heart on her the day he met her and never relented in following through; she had resisted him, but his gentle perseverance finally won her over.

Tony called to excuse himself and Elvira from dinner—although Tracy had addressed her, not him, when she invited them. Some lame reason he gave barely disguised the motive I suspected, which was to block Elvira's access to broader social circles in which he'd be less able to exert a controlling influence over her. Tracy shared my assessment, as his conversation with her over brunch was more like an interrogation about job and business opportunities.

"It was creepy," she said, demurely.

Alan's restaurant was called Bistro Biscayne—cheekily, because the only "French" item on the menu was the escargot. He had bought early into a soon-to-be-gentrified district that never quite took off once the Miami real estate bubble burst in 2008. He kept the business, though it was failing, as a gathering place for friends and family when the occasion arose, and as an art gallery for young bohemians who displayed their works on the walls. One of them was Miloš, a Czech painter who showed up with Erica, his stunning Jamaican girlfriend.

Erica made jewelry that she sold on the beach and various street markets. Her designs were colorful, whimsical, and she gave Silvia a bracelet. She had a sweet, happy disposition, like the nurse at the hospital when Silvia had her gallstone attack. I hadn't met many people from the British Caribbean, but I was beginning to notice certain common traits. Erica, however, topped the charts in terms of sheer sensual exuberance, from the sleek, sinewy flow of her endless black legs to the smoky caramel cream of her voice.

Miami was getting to be a bit much.

Alan alternated between the table and the kitchen, teaming up with his Haitian chef, with whom he communicated in French, to produce an endless flow of sage-rubbed salmon and a Creole lasagna that was the house specialty, Henri's original creation. The table was dotted with bowls of seared asparagus tips, crab-stuffed mushrooms and an artichoke-lobster dip that vied for cholesterol content with Mr. Mancini's recipes from two nights earlier.

There was a simple, honest *vin de pays* that Alan had found in Provence and kept bringing out bottle after bottle. Occasionally he sat across the table from me, next to Tracy, eyeing me intently for minutes at a time. He seemed interested in my gestures, my manner of address. Being a bit tipsy, I asked outright what was going on. "You remind him of Daddy," Tracy explained, using the childhood nickname by which we still referred to our father, even in Spanish. Alan had met him shortly before his death, and they had hit it off famously.

Daddy would have enjoyed the wine.

There were at least twenty people, and I knew barely half of them. I asked Tracy and she told me that some were regular patrons, and that they often had these open nights where everybody would mingle at the table. Sometimes they brought in musicians and would clear the middle floor for dancing. She and Alan treated everyone like family and became good friends with many. A unique business model, I thought, that Alan must have learned abroad; he had meant for the

Bistro to be a trendsetter in a neighborhood renaissance that never happened.

Miloš and Erica left early, and I couldn't help but wonder, after Thursday night's experience with Angela and her husband, why men in the company of such incredibly beautiful women so often seem to be in a bad mood. I turned to the conversations around me, dipping in and out of them like a hummingbird, on the wings of Alan's *vin de pays.* Silvia had been chatting with Erica, who spoke a little Spanish; then my niece Denise sat next to her and they were talking up a storm. We basked in the warmth of a perfect evening.

I-95

I awoke the next morning to the gentle pressure of Silvia's right arm wrapped around my chest, that she caressed with the lightest rippling motion of her fingers, as if playing *pianissimo.* Pretending still to be asleep, so as not to disrupt the delicate sweetness of the moment, I felt her naked breasts against my back as she pulled in tighter, pressing her pubic mound against my bottom. I drew my right leg forward and hers dropped into position over my left one, against which her warm wetness began to rub slowly, or rather glide back and forth.

Ahh, geometry...

She picked up the pace and was humping my leg ferociously when I rolled over and turned her under me, face up, in one continuous motion. She kept her eyes closed but her smile was sheer delight as I drove far inside her, as if spearing her all the way through. Her climax was such that my seminal fluid rushed into her seemingly drawn by her cunt, not ejected by me—a single orgasm *between* us. This is how lovemaking should always be, I felt, and pelted her with light, dry kisses on her eyelids, earlobes and the corners of her mouth, curled into a dreamy pout.

Elvira made us yet another scrumptious breakfast and within an hour we were on the road. Cruising north along the Atlantic we exchanged impressions of our recent experiences, and I was gratified that Silvia's so closely matched my own, particularly regarding the more colorful characters on the Miami stage. She liked the people I liked (including Angela), disliked the ones I didn't, extracted my penis from my pants, sucked it heartily, and made me ejaculate for the first time while driving a car, doing ninety on a laser-straight stretch of the Interstate. Such a curious way of changing the subject.

We'd had trouble, but I was still in love. Before we married she had promised me she'd fuck me forever, whenever I wanted, however frequently, even if she didn't quite feel like it. She was living up to her promise (though she did, in fact, feel *quite* like it), for it wasn't even noon and she'd done me twice already. As the landscape flew by, we alternated playing with her *mons veneris,* the orgasmatron inside her somehow coupled to the odometer. A state of permanent arousal was becoming, as I'd always wanted, our default setting.

But it was too good to be true. I had to work the next day so we made few rest stops and snacked on potato chips to make time, both of us forgetting the ill effect of hunger on her mood. Around eight at night we found a dubious buffet diner off the highway and went in for one of the worst meals I've ever had. I gave her the car keys on the way out but her driving was so erratic that I had to stop her, and she stormed out of the vehicle in the middle of an on-ramp to I-95.

"Come on, Silvia," I attempted to reason. "You can't walk home from here."

"Don't you *ever* yell at me," she railed, though, in fairness, I'd only raised my voice in panic because she'd made a right turn onto the wrong side of a divided road, ignoring or perhaps misunderstanding my instruction to turn onto the ramp just past it, and then, to correct her mistake, attempted to make a U-turn without enough room to complete it and got stuck sideways across two lanes of approaching traffic. "Leave me alone," she snarled at me, refusing to return to the car. I decided simply to wait there quietly, however long it took for her to blow off steam.

She'd done crazy things before, but I really didn't think she'd hitchhike from South Carolina, even if her anger had been justified, so I put the thought out of my mind, relaxed, and eventually dozed off. I woke up to the thud of a closing door, and turned to find her sitting in the back seat. "Are you going to stay there?" I asked her, but she wouldn't say a word. I started the car and resumed travel, content at least that nothing worse had happened. After a while I saw that she was sleeping, and stopped briefly to cover her with my coat.

It was snowing in Leesburg when we arrived around four in the morning. I'd made good time, in spite of the weather and Silvia's roadside tantrum. She went straight upstairs while I unloaded our baggage from the car, and when I came to join her she was already asleep, or pretending to be, facing away from me. She had placed the sham pillows in the middle of the bed, between my side and hers, as a "no trespassing" sign against possible advances. She adopted this practice increasingly over time, simply as a technique to deny me sex. I called it the "Berlin Wall."

For the life of me I couldn't understand how that one minor incident in South Carolina could have completely wiped out all the good feelings from the experiences we'd shared in Miami, as if she'd suddenly snapped out of a dream. Some of those experiences hadn't been so good, but we had accepted them good-naturedly and could laugh about them afterward together. Besides, it was her idea to go there in the first place, not mine; I was simply doing her bidding. Dinner with Tracy and Alan was an unexpected bonus, yet definitely a highlight of the trip, and Silvia seemed to have enjoyed it very much.

I had the unsettling notion that when she had too much fun she felt guilty about it, or perhaps resentful that she'd missed that earlier in her life. She refused to talk about it so I couldn't explore whatever reasons she had for reacting that way. I often felt that she needed help, but she'd reject that out of hand, simplistically claiming that mental health professionals are all just quacks who work on other people's problems because they can't deal with their own—after all, she'd remind me, she had taken psychology, too, in social work school. "You're right," I'd say, to humor her, but also remembering a psychiatrist acquaintance who had committed suicide.

The most worrisome area in which her moody duality came up, of course, was sex. Though she clearly attained deep catharsis when she unleashed the sexual energy I had always sensed was bottled up inside her, between such moments of wanton abandon the beautiful, free and sensual "slut" she celebrated becoming turned into a filthy whore that she loathed, or rather loathed me for leading her down that path.

There were two Silvias: one of them was crazy about me and wanted nothing better than to fuck me all the time.

But the other one...

Our interaction over spring and summer could be characterized as civil. Silvia was building a routine around her job caring for Nathan, her evening English lessons and working out at the gym. She had made friends there, including an Italian flight attendant who would pay her for helping with her garden and gave her basil cuttings to grow in our back yard. To assuage her financial concerns—although many of our problems clearly stemmed from frivolous expenditures by or for her—I began to look for a better job in the federal system.

As a federally certified interpreter I received regular notices of vacancies around the country, which I'd previously ignored, having no desire to move. But Lizzie was in college and Chris would soon be, too, so it didn't matter where I lived anymore. For the same work I was doing in Virginia, the federal courts paid double, and the administrative skills I'd picked up at this job, plus my overall interpreting experience, made me eligible for one of those positions. It was a logical next step for me, but mostly I just wanted to make Silvia happy.

When she'd been in Bogotá she had relocated her daughters to her sister Catalina's house and put her own apartment up for rent to help support them. Her other sisters seemed intent on feeding her bad news about Verónica and Marcela, particularly the former's constant clashes with her aunt, who made them follow strict house rules that Silvia never taught them, and Catalina herself did not enforce on her own daughter Vicky. The Morales girls had become Cinderellas; it was a kind of soap opera whose only real effect was to keep Silvia constantly on the phone.

Putting myself in her place, it seemed to me that if my husband had seduced my sister's daughter, I wouldn't be sending my own daughters to live with both the aunt who probably still resented that and the cousin whose child might be their brother. But then Silvia's brother by adoption was actually her nephew, because when Sara, her oldest sister, got knocked up at age fifteen, their mother helped her hide the pregnancy from their father and brought the baby into the home as a foundling.

Appearances, for *rolos,* are everything.

In fact, at times I thought that all of our communication problems could be traced to that particular persuasion. During my college years in Cali we could always tell when someone was a *rolo* if, in a public bus, they were standing and a passenger seated next to them rose to leave, freeing the seat. The *rolo* would turn around and sort of hover his arse over the empty seat, to claim it, but only actually sit down after a prudent time had passed. It was as if they might catch something from the body heat of the previous passenger and had to let it dissipate.

The first time I visited Bogotá with some *Caleño* friends we howled with laughter when we saw that *everybody* did that. At a busy stop you could board a bus and see half the passengers in that ludicrous crouching stance, straining their quadriceps to delay their butt's contact with the seat. The time it took them to drop down was a measure of their sophistication and they competed sullenly, without a sideward glance, to outsquat one another. They could even read a newspaper in that position, taking the ridiculous to the height of the sublime.

I never could quite convince Silvia that it really was OK to eat chicken wings with her fingers. I adduced scientific proof that going at a hamburger with knife and fork misses the point of that most American of inventions, which, by surrounding the meat and fixings with two halves of a bun, allows the eater to hold it with one hand, without dripping grease and ketchup all over himself, while driving the car or answering the phone with the other. It seemed to me that her full sexual liberation required some grasp of these concepts.

But seriously, her stilted adherence to vacuous formalities was a formidable barrier to the open-mindedness required to build a new life with a new person in a new country. The priority she gave to saving face over letting go of old paradigms, pretending to already know things she'd never been exposed to before, biased her toward a defensive and ultimately hostile posture. A full two weeks after a light-hearted quip I made about the "upside-down" label on the new wide-capped ketchup bottles, she revealed it had offended her. "I *knew* that," she muttered.

The subtler experiences of life didn't stand a chance against such entrenchment. I, who had never taken anything seriously unless it were truly a matter of life or death (or maybe love, which can be either), only knew to deal with it by further making light of the circumstances that brought about such misunderstandings—the definition, for me, of a joke. But she wasn't laughing, and I was at a loss. Our lovemaking was less frequent, and acquired the furtive, groping quality of mutual masturbation. It was increasingly clear that we were drifting apart.

Reinforcements

"The visas came through," Silvia announced one day, without so much as cracking a smile. After the importance she'd given to bringing Verónica and Marcela to the States, I'd half expected she'd lapse into a giddy euphoria, perhaps even throw herself around my neck. But no, it simply had to happen; it came from God. In just a few months the girls would finish their semesters and fly to mommy. Lizzie wasn't using her room, so they could have it. Everything was going to work out. At least the phone bill would come down, I hoped.

Verónica arrived in September to a crisp autumn breeze. Restless in nature, her attention jumped from object to object and she reacted to her new environs in cascades of running comment with which she attempted to match everything to a preset matrix in her mind. Living there, I imagined, must have been a little like hallucinating. Her random questions sought not so much answers as validation of theories and conjectures with which she'd already explained an unfamiliar cultural landscape to herself—in other words, she was opinionated.

The intellectual self-sufficiency with which she fabricated knowledge had been a boon to her in college, and in Leesburg she leveraged that skill into better and better employment opportunities. The first job she took was at the same restaurant where Silvia had worked for a while, but she quickly surpassed her mother in responsibilities and pay, which she doubled overnight by becoming a waitress. Her English was effective enough, having attended a bilingual school in Bogotá, and her eager attentiveness to patrons won her handsome tips.

Her goal was to return to college, but until she'd been a resident for at least a year she'd be paying astronomical tuition as a foreign student, and her English wasn't as good as she thought. Comparing herself to native speakers, especially at the college level, she realized that she had a fair amount of work ahead, and she'd have to take the Test of English as a Foreign Language (TOEFL) to be admitted. She undertook to do so promptly and got a full-time day job at Wellmark so that she could take evening classes. Soon she was a supervisor.

When Marcela arrived in November (her semester was on a different calendar) her sister got her a job at the same store, and within a few weeks they were functioning as a coordinated production unit, quite in spite of the employment doldrums nationwide. Silvia was proud of both of them and so was I, because their earnest zeal would soon enable them to overcome the heavy setback that their father had dealt them, for which I felt, if not guilty, at least partly responsible.

But they felt otherwise.

Just to be sure that we were all on the same page I went over the college situation, reiterating that *we*—their mother and I—had originally intended that they finish college in Colombia and join us later, whether for employment or postgraduate options. The fact that we had to scramble to get them back on track was due to Major Morales's unexpected withdrawal of support, I hoped they realized. What Silvia told them, though, must have been something else; I never knew exactly what, but their attitude told me that they held me accountable for the crisis.

Nevertheless, over time a workable rapport developed, which I reinforced with outings to places of interest and an avid interest in their assimilation. Both girls had Colombian driver's licenses that they converted to Virginia licenses as soon as their green cards came in. Within a couple of months they enjoyed an independence and freedom of movement that their mother had failed to attain in over a year. She began leaning on them for everything she used to get from me. They had the car full-time, as my job was within walking distance.

Unlike Verónica and her mother, Marcela enrolled in an English immersion course offered by the same community college Silvia had been to. She juggled her hours at Wellmark in order to attend the full-strength, TOEFL-specific program. Her adaptation technique, while not as bold as her sister's, was more systematic and sure-footed. Also, she was only three semesters into college, whereas Verónica had completed seven, so she was really looking at starting over, not one final push like the other, who planned to achieve that by joining the military.

I did what I could to keep their options open. Before Marcela's arrival, Silvia and I had taken Verónica to a Navy recruiting office. She leaned more toward the Air Force because she thought it better matched her background in aeronautical engineering (though her Colombian course descriptions looked more, to me, like aircraft maintenance); I, however, felt the Navy had a more diverse technology curriculum, and the Pensacola Naval Air Station housed a satellite campus of her dream school, Embry-Riddle Aeronautical University.

But she scored a dismal fifteen percent on a pre-admission test she took, due primarily to her non-existing grasp of technical English. They gave her a book to prepare for a later try, but it was clear that her chances were slim even for enlisted admission, and without a college degree she couldn't aspire to officer school in either the Air Force or the Navy. Since the whole point of joining was to get said degree in the first place, she was faced with a Catch-22. She needed to bring her English up several notches, and make a living in the meantime.

Marcela had a completely different approach. She didn't "Americanize" her pronunciation as much as Verónica (who did so mostly to sound "cool"), but focused on construction and comprehension, making little effort to mask the Spanish accent that both girls had, albeit in different measure. We visited several Washington area universities that could help her with a double major in political science and international studies. After quick looks at American, Georgetown and George Washington, she decided she liked George Mason best.

It was also the most realistic choice. As a Virginia resident, she'd benefit from the most comprehensive financial aid options, and the various academic offices we visited persuaded Marcela that GMU could build her the closest approximation of her envisioned plan of study. I was unabashed in my zeal to connect her to the campus community, and introduced her to foreign students on sight, thinking that such conversations would give her the best sense of what the school was like. A girl from Panama, a senior, offered to help.

Snow

Winter came early in 2010: it started snowing in November. Silvia's daughters had never been in the snow before, so I gave them two shovels and sent them outside to enjoy it. At their ages, they were in much better shape than I was, yet they tired easily so I had to don my gloves and winter coat, anyway, to finish digging out the car in time for them to get to work. For that reason I had abandoned for some time already my earlier rapt enchantment with snow, a noun that I'd more recently taken to embellishing with the prefix "fucking."

But I still had fond memories of a monster snowstorm years before when the precipitation was measured in feet, not inches, and Chris and Lizzie had built a huge snow fort in the front yard. Just like them, Verónica and Marcela came back into the house with ruddy bright cheeks and a zesty appetite for hot cocoa and Colombian *arepas* their mom made for them. I couldn't deprive them of the grand American tradition of snowmen and snowball fights, so I instructed them in the proper manner of making and waging, respectively, each.

I had my own family tradition of skidding the car in snow-covered empty parking lots, a technique I had perfected with a rear-wheel-drive pick-up truck I used to own and could spin in a circle with the front wheels stationary in the center, for the squealing amusement of my children. But when I tried it with Silvia and her daughters, who were sitting in the back seat, we slammed sideways into a hidden divider and their heads knocked together with a loud *thunk.* They wobbled dizzily out of the car as I apologized profusely.

The car wobbled, too, as we embarked on a much-humbled homeward retreat, limping pitifully like a three-legged dog. The rear axle was bent and I had to spend thirteen hundred dollars to fix it. I wanted to take them to the hospital to check for possible concussion but they insisted they were OK—all they wanted was my promise that I'd never take them snow drifting again. They thanked their lucky stars that the car had not turned over. As in so many other noble purposes, my effort to show them some fun had gone seriously awry.

This backfiring of good intentions became the bane of my existence as I sought to provide a home for the three Colombian women I'd brought into my life as the result of marrying one. The power once went out because I forgot to pay the bill, so I got them plastic flashlights—Verónica's was green; Marcela's, orange—with which they made spooky faces by lighting them from below, in the same good-humored spirit with which my own children had weathered minor hardships in the past: occasional mishaps would become opportunities for play.

But Silvia was seething, mostly because she had given her daughters a completely different impression of what our life was like before they were forced to join us. "But, Ma" (Verónica always called her "Ma," in a babyish whine), "you never told us Danny had so many problems." She'd never told them many things, but now, in the spirit of full disclosure, she told them everything, including that our Cartagena honeymoon had been her idea, not mine, and that I'd only paid for half of the four million pesos it had cost. I'd always suspected as much; in retrospect, it was obvious.

Silvia had been aware that I didn't have $2,000 for the trip, after scrimping to make ends meet for the marriage to come about, yet she felt that I should pay *something*, husband that I was, and didn't want me to know about her tidy cash reserve, after all her bellyaching about my remittances. She told the girls that she'd kept the truth from them hoping that things would improve before they came, but it didn't happen as we'd planned—which proved to them precisely what she'd previously denied: that my intention had always been to bring them to the States.

Before Verónica and Marcela came to live with us, every Saturday Silvia would ask me to take her to a flea market where used clothing and household goods were sold for pennies on the dollar. We also went to thrift shops and the Salvation Army store, where she bought me two good suits for ten dollars each. Hand-me-downs in this affluent area were top quality, almost new. Silvia delighted in assembling care packages for her sisters, nieces and nephews, but when the girls arrived she was adamant that I shouldn't mention any of that to them.

It perplexed me that she strove so hard to maintain the illusion of a material comfort she claimed her husband had always provided them, considering how unceremoniously his generosity ended when she chose to live a life of her own, and that he had stripped his daughters of the most valuable thing he could have ever given them, a college education. Such incongruence made me wonder if the underlying story was true at all, or she was simply lying; but I had to accept that some things must always remain private, even within the bounds of marriage.

As our ties continued to unravel, she pressed more insistently against those bounds, and again brought up the issue of divorce. Her freedom was important to her, she said, and I'd promised that I'd never take it away from her. I couldn't do that if I tried, I pointed out, and repeated my belief that a spousal commitment is not an infringement of freedom, but rather a way of leveraging the freedom of a loving couple to achieve together a happiness unattainable individually by each. All of that, to her, was empty rhetoric.

She simply wanted out, regardless of whether or not she loved me, an issue that she'd skirt with red herrings: "If I didn't love you I wouldn't have left Colombia, where I was comfortable and had everything." Or: "If I didn't love you, I wouldn't have fucked you like I did last night." If, if... Why was it so difficult to simply say, "I love you?" There was the rub: if she said that, and it were true, why divorce me? A divorce, she claimed, would make her free to love me for myself, not out of formal obligation. I thought a job was a better way of accomplishing that.

Silvia made much of the semantically trivial distinction between *amar* and *querer,* both meaning "to love," but the first, from the Latin *amare,* almost exclusively of literary use; it sounds stilted and contrived in common speech. The second, from *quaerere*—closer in literal meaning to "to want"—is standard Colombian usage for all permutations of love: romantic, filial, fraternal... I merely "wanted" her but didn't "love" her, she claimed, to disqualify my feelings as part of her argument that I wasn't, though her husband, the man of her life.

The man that God had promised her would truly love her, not just want her, like me, as shown by my preference for saying "*te quiero*" instead of "*te amo.*" And it was already too late to do anything about it—I should have thought of that before she made up the rule, not as a correction after the fact, just to please her; that wouldn't be sincere. Nor possible: pleasing her was a labor of Sisyphus, with ever-changing requirements I could never ponder, much less meet. So God gave her license to move on, to find the perfect lover He meant for her since the beginning of time.

I shuddered when she began a sentence with "honestly," because I knew I was in for a whopper. Though I propounded a notion of freedom built on partnering to achieve together what was individually out of our reach, strengthened by the body-soul replenishment of sexual satisfaction, bla bla bla, the freedom she sought was *from* the relationship, and she expressed it by an increasing emotional distance from me— which by no means diminished, however, *my* obligations. Commitment, to her, was tantamount to enslavement: not something freely given, but exacted from others.

A cold anomie crept into every aspect of our life. Breakfast, lunch, dinner and every daily function slowly acquired the gray drudgery of tedious routine. She'd often leave in the evening, vaguely mentioning unclear social commitments that she'd return from late and go to bed without a word as I pretended to sleep, so as not to argue. Our sex life was a shambles. There was hardly any when the girls were around, and when there was she was more concerned with hushing any telltale signs of lovemaking than with fully enjoying the occasion.

During one such encounter, perched astride me, she was causing me uncomfortable penile bending and compression. "What are you doing?" I asked. "I want to put it in my ass," she said, but her placement was off, plus no lubrication. She gave up on that and took me vaginally, but slamming all her weight down on my stomach; gone were the tight pelvic swing and on-axis balance she'd worked so hard to perfect—her physical intelligence. I flipped her and took her from behind, but as I emptied myself into her she wasn't pleased; that wasn't what she had in mind.

We were increasingly out of synch. She was merely going through the motions, uninspired, frustrated that it wasn't working. One day I was engaged with her in oral foreplay while kneading her tumid breasts and she clutched my hands firmly in hers, making me squeeze her nipples so hard I was concerned that I might cause her damage. Her pain/pleasure threshold had evidently shifted upward, and it struck me that she'd never expressed such a preference before. I obliged her but was curious where it came from. "Víctor," she said, distractedly.

We last made love as a married couple during the great blizzard of 2010. It had been snowing for days. The steady windblown stream, as seen through the window, made it seem as though we hurtled swiftly forth across vast white expanses. She was supple, with a graceful air that had been missing for some time. I climaxed in a smooth, effortless segue to the precise pivot action with which she met my full thrusts, curling slightly at the bottom, her pelvic tilt a perfect match to the angle of penetration, which she optimized by locking her chest down on the bed.

It was beautiful, but I was distressed, melancholic. "I will always remember this time," I told her, and she wanted to know why. "I don't know... the snow, the silence outside. Maybe the way your body looked just now, the inward arch of your back... it's my favorite position." But I knew better: it was a mercy fuck, full of sadness. I could sense the growing distance, a separation between the sensual urge and a deeper yearning for togetherness, completeness. We lingered briefly, but lacking altogether the ethereal languor we used to enjoy post-coitus; it had flown away.

She got up to wash. As she walked across the room she covered her breasts with her arms. I never could understand the prudish affectation with which she guarded some misplaced notion of decorum, hiding from my gaze the very riches she had just surrendered to me moments before. A *rola* thing, I'd often thought, but I was beginning to understand what it really meant: that she wasn't mine, and never had or would be. My sense of betrayal continued to build, and the despair of abandonment settled ever more deeply in my heart.

When the girls returned Silvia did her best to remain aloof, thereby reassuring them that our afternoon together had been nothing but a few empty hours of humdrum domestic coexistence. She addressed me politely, as if talking to a nameless clerk in some public office. Before long she moved into the girls' room, first under the guise that being with them was a much-deserved reward for having waited so long to be together, but eventually as a clear statement that we simply wouldn't be sleeping together, that we weren't a couple anymore. They were looking for a place of their own, she casually mentioned once, as if nothing could be more natural.

I took to watching TV. I couldn't find anything at first, and even when I mustered the interest to stay tuned to one of the hundreds of empty channels, the witless inanity of endless commercials was almost too much to bear, but for the wordless alienation I faced in the house. Silvia's indifference was painful, but I knew I couldn't plead for sympathy without setting off her ruthless browbeating. "Respect isn't something you demand," she'd preach; "you have to earn it." It was pointless to ask when or how I'd lost it; I'd never had it.

"All I ever get from you is disdain," I'd occasionally complain, as if an awareness of her destructive attitude might prompt her to adopt at least a semblance of appreciation for any good I may had brought into her life. But she was well aware of her attitude; indeed, she prized it, and affirmed it with a quiet smirk that said, "Yeah, you got that right." I began to realize—slowly, because I was still hopeful—that the pain she caused me pleased her, and my sadness shrouded itself in anger. I began to seethe.

Out!

One Monday in March she marched into the bedroom with a scowl that irked me, because we hadn't had any fights all weekend and it seemed gratuitous, even by her arbitrary standards. "What's the matter?" I asked. "You," she snapped back. "What did I do now? How can we fix it? We can't just go on like this, enemies under the same roof, constantly tearing each other apart." She gave me a withering, stone-cold look. "Do whatever you want," she sneered, and I exploded: "You miserable wretch! Just leave me, already. Get out of my fucking house."

I bolted. As I opened the door Marcela was standing in the hallway, somewhat like that first night in Bogotá, now taking in an entirely different facet of our relationship. "I have to get out," I told her, as calmly as I could, because it pained me to upset her, the more sensitive of the three, the only one who had made an effort to understand. She seemed to sense that her mother was unfair, and that the derision she heaped on me did not entirely stem from my failings, real or perceived, but from a fundamental dishonesty that had nothing to do with me.

I put no stock in these inklings of loyalty; blood is thicker than water and I knew that she'd side with her mom, of course, if push ever came to shove, which push was fast approaching. I went to work, steaming all morning. At lunch I came home, and the three of them were eating at the table.

"What, you're not gone yet?" I was intent on staying angry, because I thought it would protect me from further abuse. Yes, I'd become the abuser, I thought. I had nothing to lose. That was already how she treated me, and it wasn't going to stop.

The same scene repeated itself on Wednesday, but Silvia asked me if I'd like to join them for lunch. "OK, I'm tired of being angry," I said, and I really was; it was beginning to feel phony. Maybe we could still work things out. I was glad to drop the huffy, indignant persona and be myself again for a while. I might even not watch TV that evening, and give civil discourse with my wife and stepdaughters another chance. That fickle, flickering light of hope tickled at my heart again and softened my resolve to act in my own best interest, alas.

Life hobbled along, communication at the bare minimum for basic household coordination. The girls requested a meeting, and I agreed to sit down with the three of them after work. A lady from Bolivia had offered to rent them a room. Did I want them to leave, or was some kind of accommodation still possible? They were welcome to stay, I told them, but Marcela went into a rant about how poorly I was treating her mother. Her father, whatever else might be said about him, was a *gentleman,* she claimed, and had always treated Silvia with respect.

"If you're expecting a fast guarantee that I'll never have another argument with your mother, then it may be better if you leave," I said.

"It's settled, then," Verónica answered. "That's all we needed to know."

"We're leaving tomorrow," added Silvia. I stood up and went to bed, dozing off as their talk continued downstairs. I was weary, and it was done. They'd made up their minds, and there was nothing I could do about it. They wanted my capitulation, not a solution, but I stood my ground. I'd be alone, I realized, but the strife would end.

I was numb as I left for work the following morning, expecting to return to an empty home. But at lunchtime Silvia was still there with Marcela. "Can we talk?" she asked after eating, but I was running late. Marcela offered to drive me to the courthouse, and began to thank me, as I exited the car, for having "taken care" of their mother. I interrupted her: "How dare you compare me to your father? Habitually fucking whores and then coming home to stick the same filthy dick in your mother's body... that's *respect?* Which one of you is the dumbest?"

Her pain was deep, sharp, and instant. She let out a pitiful belly sob as I slammed the door. Of the three, I had always had the highest regard for Marcela, and now I had emptied all my pain on her. But she had betrayed me, too, just like Verónica, and their mother. Once they went into battle formation, I didn't have the slightest chance of regaining any semblance of a marriage; the only outcome they'd have accepted would have been unconditional surrender. I felt bad about hurting her, but I couldn't help it—I was overcome by a crippling darkness.

When I arrived to an empty house after work that day, I began sobbing inconsolably almost as soon as I closed the door behind me. I was bereft. Silvia had barely left, and already her over-the-top offensive tirades seemed preferable to the gnawing, wrenching agony of letting her go. Over the following days I would sit for hours staring blankly into the air, in a grueling tug-of-war with the pain that threatened to take my mind over completely.

All I could think of after smoking a cigarette was to light another one. But I stood fast.

Then I began to take stock of my year-and-a-half experience living with Silvia and then her daughters. I had pushed every other interest, every other relationship, out of my life. I'd become a shadow father, nodding perfunctorily to acknowledge Chris's occasional appearances at home, when he ran out of friends to "hang out" with. Lizzie, declared *persona non grata* by Silvia, remained safely away at college, and walked on eggshells whenever she dropped by, always briefly. I would no longer have to choose between daughter and wife.

Or rather, I had chosen. But the pain lingered, and festered. Even as my rational brain congratulated me for having done the right thing, my emotions continued to torture me with memories of paradise lost: Bogotá, Cartagena, Cancún. Was I to live the rest of my life without the mad rush of those high-energy passages? Was I to renounce Guantánamo? I broke down in the car with Lizzie one day. "I'm still in love with Silvia," I explained to her, embarrassed at dragging my daughter into my "pity party," as she called it. "Oh, stop it, dad," she said. "She already has a boyfriend."

I was thunderstruck. "What are you talking about? How do you know?" Her mom had seen them holding hands in a parking lot, she explained. Apparently everybody knew but me. "He's a *gringo*. A pretty old one, too," Lizzie added, disgusted both at Silvia's sleaze and my own craven self-delusion. My stomach began to turn and I considered pulling over to throw up, but managed not to. All the elements of reality swirled around in a tornado that reconfigured every past perception. Silvia was no longer who I thought she was, nor her daughters.

Molière had summed it up in *Tartuffe:* "We are most easily deceived by those we love." Now it all made sense: girls' nights out with friends who wouldn't pick her up at the door, but meet her around the corner; that sudden drop in her sexual IQ. I'd always been skeptical of the obvious, because it got in the way of the profound; that was also, however, a good way of fooling myself. Now the profound was obvious: I was the new Víctor, but I'd been defeated, and a new Daniel was raking in my chips. Self-pity gave way to jealousy, and rage.

I'd already been through Silvia's lies and deception, but wrote them off as pious equivocation, a necessary corollary to her self-righteous façade as a spotless, proper *rola*. I didn't judge her hypocrisy too harshly; she dissembled to protect her self-esteem. But I hadn't yet felt jealousy, the sulfuric acid of love; nor the burning sting of treason—the sin, according to Dante, of the bottommost denizens of hell. Suddenly, I remembered that she'd come home one night, well before her daughters arrived, with a Spanish-English dictionary that an "old man" had given her.

I didn't have long to wait to meet him. They were sitting at the middle table in the Four Leaf Clover, an Irish pub where I used to take her, as I walked in one evening for a drink. "Hi, Daniel. I'm Dirk," he said, stretching out his hand when she introduced us. He made no effort to sit up from his sprawled-out position on the seat, cowboy boots jutting out on the other side of the table. "Nice to meet you," I lied, continuing quickly to my usual spot toward the end of the bar. I ordered my drink and went to the bathroom. I felt an irresistible urge to wash my hands.

As I returned, Silvia was standing in the narrow walkway between the restrooms and the main floor. "He's just a friend," she pleaded. "Looks more like an orangutan to me," I spat back. "An old one, too. Besides, aren't you all footloose and fancy-free now? Why give me any explanations?" She persisted: "But he's just a friend. There's nothing between us." Right... just holding hands, that's all. "There's nothing between us, either, so go 'hang out' with your orangutan," I said. "He's *not* an orangatoon," she fretted. "He's a nice man. Plus, he has a girlfriend. She's from the Philippines."

So they were *double* two-timers. I eyed them with loathing, like cockroaches, from the bar. She sat, prim and proper, back straight up as per *rola* etiquette, preening her antennae, glancing restlessly about as Dirk watched a football game on the large screen behind the counter. Not a word between them—perforce, unless he spoke Spanish (unlikely) or she had memorized that dictionary already. He looked so smug and she so lost that pity crept into my disgust: what pathetic, vain delusion could she be feeding by latching on to the first vapid *gringo* she ran into?

The chronic turning of my stomach—a new trait I had developed—told me it was time to leave. "Let me know how the game goes, Silvia," I tossed at her in passing after leaving my tip at the bar. "So long, Dick," I added, hoping he wouldn't answer. He obliged me partly with a vague, grunting sound. I couldn't make it out, but whatever he said was far less important than the game, that absorbed his full attention. I could have tied Silvia up and hauled her off in a wheelbarrow, and he probably wouldn't have noticed until halftime.

I was still in touch with the girls, for in spite of everything I had assumed with them a caretaker role, perfected over twelve years as a single father, rearing children that meant everything to me. Like those dogs that raise tiger cubs, the habit simply carried over to anyone I considered my responsibility, whether they deserved it or not. In the case of Silvia's litter I was genuinely interested in their future, having been so close to recent misadventures in their past. By the same token, I felt they owed me some consideration.

"He's just a friend," said Verónica, parroting her mom, when I asked her who this Dirk was. Separately, Marcela said she didn't know him. They were covering up for Silvia, but hadn't squared their story. Sandra tipped me off to a baby blue Volkswagen they were driving those days. They stopped by my office to pick up their mail and I offered to walk them to the car, but they didn't want me to. I followed them anyway and saw the Beetle —ingeniously tagged BEEDL, on foxhunting vanity plates. Dirk wasn't any old cowboy; he was an *anglophile* cowboy.

I abhorred this cowardly sport* with which moneyed Piedmont philistines ape the lordly ways of the odious redcoats our forefathers pledged their lives, fortune and sacred honor to rid us of. Such sad irony, that the most perfervid blatherers of glib Americana, the "patriots" who dragged us into Iraq looking for non-existing weapons of mass destruction, and into Afghanistan for terrorists who were in Pakistan, should fawn over the idle, genteel lifestyle that Franklin, Swift and Paine lampooned so richly: the spoor of Perfidious Albion.

But then, what could these lost, ambitious Colombian girls know about what it really means to be an *American?* They'd landed a live one—give or take a few billion neurons—and weren't about to fret over cultural-historical quibbles. I could see it now: I had been a stepping-stone to a greater good,

---

* Now banned in Scotland, England and Wales.

to the lofty goal of "hooking them up" with a solid exponent of the true-blue, unadulterated *gringo*-ness they'd seen on television. They had it made, they must have figured, and any small discomfort along the way was simply the price to pay... by others.

I remembered the cab ride to the ferry dock on the way to Isla Mujeres. The driver, an affable Oaxacan, wanted to know where we were from. "I'm from Colombia," said Silvia, proudly. "And you, sir?" he asked. "Me too," I answered, but she recoiled viscerally: "No, you're not! You're *American!*" She seemed embarrassed to be seen, even by a perfect stranger, with anyone but a thoroughbred *gringo,* a pedigree that in me was tarnished by the very national heritage that she'd just boasted as a mark of distinction. She didn't want a man; she wanted status.

I didn't blame her, then or later; she was burdened by her past. Most of the time I just blamed myself, convinced that none of this would be happening if I hadn't been such a screw-up. And Dirk was, after all, "just a friend," so who was I to deny Silvia her First Amendment right to associate with any slimy creep she chose to? I waited after church one Sunday. She fell behind the others as they came out, and approached me with a sheepish grin. "So when do I get to see you?" she asked, sending waves of cognitive dissonance ricocheting inside my skull.

'Bro'

Dirk was sitting in the first booth on my right as I entered the Four Leaf Clover a few days later. I sat opposite, toward the end of the bar, and could see him out of the corner of my eye: beer, BlackBerry, laptop and cigar in an orderly array that defined a kind of territory. I walked over and asked if we could have a word. "Sure, Daniel. I'm just finishing something up right now, but if you'll give me a minute..." Important guy. I had the notion that people who bring work to places of entertainment are essentially phony.

"I'll wait at the bar," I said.

He switched from his computer to his BlackBerry, then put it away and waved me over. "Would you like a cigar?" he offered. He carried several kinds in a sandwich bag, and made a big deal of choosing the right one for me to smoke. As he fumbled, I studied his face, looking for signs of character, but his dull, gray eyes, sunken and close-set across a straight, strong nose, gave little sign of life. He had a chiseled, inexpressive look, like those blond action figures that exterminate swarthy aliens, but graying. "Here, try this one. I think you'll like it.

"What can I do for you, Daniel?" I sensed condescension at once. "Well, you know Silvia's my wife, and we've been having a rough time." I had no idea what to say. "Yes. You're separated, in fact." How perceptive. "Exactly. But married still, and I want her back. I'd like to know what *your* intentions are. How serious are you about Silvia?" Might as well be blunt. He eyed me comically, though not intentionally so. "We're just friends, Daniel. She's a fine woman, very well behaved." Whatever that meant, he sounded like a dog show judge.

I gave him something to chew on, information that Silvia would have withheld from him. "Have you met the daughters?" I asked. I didn't expect it, but that triggered an involuntary reflex: a cold, lecherous gleam from the bottom of his frozen gaze: "Yeah. Verónica's quite striking, isn't she? A real princess..." He checked himself, but I'd seen enough. "I'm more fond of Marcela," I said. "She's the smarter, more sensitive of the two."

He changed the subject: "So how can I help you with your conundrum, bro?" No question: I was dealing with an asshole.

"I don't know, Dirk. What does a guy say to someone who's seeing his wife? Put yourself in my shoes. What would you do?" It didn't make him uncomfortable in the least. Timing himself to sound cool, he paused thoughtfully and drew on his cigar, letting the full impact of his advantageous position sink in. "Sometimes you just have to ride these things out, bro. Give it some time, see if it works out later, a couple of months, maybe." Fucking bastard. "Yeah, I guess you're right. Well, I can see you're busy. Thanks for the cigar," I said. "No problem, bro."

I wanted to ask him Silvia's darkest secret: how they had met, and when. Whether it was before or after moving out made all the difference: was she needy, alone, and found a sympathetic ear, or was he in fact a driving force in our estrangement, already lurking in the background? The answer would also be a measure of her dishonesty. I fondled the idea of an immigration case: if she'd married intending to dump me as soon as her visa and her daughters' cleared, she had committed fraud. But the old lizard knew that, so he wasn't going to say a word.

I never was any good at poker, so I dumped the whole story on Silvia first chance I got, with added emphasis on the dirty-old-man angle. I'd been checking Dirk out with the Clover regulars and nobody liked him, which said a lot: no friends, no casual chitchat with patrons, waitresses or bartenders. Somebody thought he was a narc, but that guy was probably a stoner, and stoners see narcs under the bed. My Pentagon buddy, however, gave me a solid lead: the BEEDL license plate was untraceable; it was blocked by Homeland Security.

"Shit! They're going after Silvia!" I thought. From past work with international law enforcement programs I was aware of informal arrangements between legal attachés and local assets, and saw a possibility that Sergio might have called in a favor to inflict macho payback on the wayward ex who wouldn't bend to his will. It was far-fetched, but possible, and certainly preferable to admitting that Silvia had simply met a common cad who didn't mind screwing around with a married woman. Affecting panic, I laid the scenario out to her.

"So they deport me," she laughed. "Big deal! I never was into this whole American Dream thing in the first place." Good parry. I'd forgotten what a deadeye haggler she was. She strengthened her position by diminishing the value of the negative consequences I presented to her. I came back stronger: "It's not that simple. In Colombia, you'd have a deportation record that would block you from getting other visas, like maybe to the European Union." That got her attention.

"So what are you saying, Daniel? What do you think is going on?"

She'd entered the country as the wife of a U.S. citizen, who also then brought her two daughters. Shortly after they arrived she moved out of her husband's home and began an affair (in that order?) with another, more affluent U.S. citizen. So, moral turpitude, immigration fraud, all that.

"But I'm not sleeping with Dirk," she protested. "Doesn't matter," I stood firm. "Have you ever kissed or even held hands in a public place, where you could be photographed? Any time alone inside a private home or lodging, where you could be filmed entering or leaving?"

"Well, yes. There was that one time we were holding hands at the mall. We were just being silly." I thought I had tricked her into coming clean, but she was smarter than that: more likely she'd spotted my ex spotting her, so she jumped at the chance to equivocate. I started hoping Dirk really *was* with ICE and they'd ship her ass back to Colombia. Indeed, it would be dereliction of duty *not* to, even —or especially—if he had entrapped her.

"That's all it takes, Silvia. Adultery is no more than 'intimacy' with someone whom you're legally barred from marrying." It didn't matter if the set-up was fair, standard or even legal, I added. If someone was out to get her, they'd find a way; all she had to give them was half a chance.

I was pretty convincing, and maybe even right. I made a note to check the facts later, but for the moment I was content with shaking her up. Also that bastard would have to work a little harder now to gain her confidence. Whether she came back to me or not, as long as it was a matter of someone else lying, cheating, and stealing what was rightfully mine, I'd fight every inch of the way.

"You were right!" she came back, within a week. "You mean, about Dirk, that he's a fed? Of course I'm right," I said. She'd asked him questions that would be answered differently by someone with or without access to law enforcement databases, and he'd actually not seen it coming when she called him on it. "So you had some fun, eh?" I wasn't really surprised, after what she'd told me about Sergio's intelligence work. "Yeah. But he's not coming after me. He really just wants to be friends." So, back to square one.

Silvia, however, was impressed that I'd helped her score one on the new guy. Her devious clockwork orange was computing an algorithm that would allow her to keep me around just for fun, and maybe the occasional grand slam that she wasn't getting from Dirk, I was inclined to believe. Whatever the actual degree of intimacy between them, whether she was lying a lot or a little (but lying, for sure), I could sense the hunger still inside her. I was still her prey but she suppressed that instinct in pursuit of a different sort of quarry.

Little Black Dress

And thus the games began... or advanced to the next stage, more precisely. Silvia was blocking her phone number from me, and they thought they were hiding their new address, but I already knew it—I was even forwarding their mail; didn't they notice? She called me often, and we'd arrange to meet somewhere, as long as the girls "didn't know." I protested that I didn't have the same freedom to contact her as she had to call me, but in due time I figured that out, too: she was using Marcela's old number, still active on my account.

Verónica and Marcela began trickling back into the picture. I'd drop their mother off surreptitiously at random locations where they'd pick her up from "errands," but one day she couldn't find them so I simply drove her home. "How come you never came here?" she puzzled. Simple: "I had no business here, and I wasn't welcome." Eventually the girls started coming along for the occasional lunch or dinner. As always, Marcela was more pleasant than Verónica, although the latter, unlike the former, didn't mind asking me to take them on outings.

One of these was to Obrycki's, in Baltimore, a crab house I had described to them with drooling reverence. I was having problems with my radiator and was leery of a long drive, but Dirk had lent them the Beedl because the Bolivian lady's van was in the shop. "Let's take Dirk's car," they said, and I felt a bit funny but, in the spirit of my new covenant with Silvia, it made a twisted sort of sense: if he was going to be seeing my wife, why shouldn't I be driving his car? Weirdly, along the way Silvia made disparaging remarks about him.

We parked by the Inner Harbor and took a water taxi to Fells Point. We walked up Broadway, taking in the sights of the bustling restaurant and entertainment district, including Bertha's, home of the world's best bumper sticker: "Eat Bertha's Mussels." We ate blue crab to our hearts' content, the girls quickly mastering the technique and putting away crab after crab with near-industrial dispatch. I drew satisfaction from seeing their enjoyment of every new experience; it was a vicarious happiness that made up for going unthanked.

For Verónica's birthday I gave her a trial flight in a Diamond DA40, a single-engine four-seater used by the local flight school. I shared her interest in aeronautics and had helped her with college papers. She had a collection of World War II die cast aircraft models that I had been sending her over the years. The three boarded the airplane and I gazed wistfully from the fence as they took off. I had always wanted to do that myself. When they landed, two hours later, the instructor praised Verónica's airworthiness, and she wanted to go to lunch.

I'd eaten already while they were aloft, so I declined her invitation to invite them. We could go to one of the local vineyards later, I suggested, when the sun was down a bit. It was a gorgeous, breezy day and I felt like a nap in my room, with the window open. Verónica had to work, but Silvia and Marcela accepted the offer. They were better company, anyway, and Verónica was already well served. Silvia could nap with me, I ventured, and we could pick Marcela up later; but Silvia "had to change," and asked me to pick both of them up at four.

I was flattered when she came down the stairs in a trim, perky Little Black Dress I'd found for her in New York. The darted midsection accentuated the taper from hip to waist (a weakness whereof she constantly bemoaned) and gave her bottom room to shift inside the fabric, further dramatizing the double action of her stride. The perfect mounds of her uplifted breasts welled up gracefully from the low horizontal neckline joining the crisply tailored quarter-sleeves that cupped her shoulders and added poise to her naturally upright bearing.

She often complimented me on my good taste and awareness of her figure, which wasn't easy to shop for, according to her. There was a strapless Allen Schwartz I had once mailed her, also tailored to increase the curviness of a fairly straight waistline, with metallic bronze, black and silver horizontal stripes on an off-white rayon background. Her friends from fashion school (another diploma she held) had told her that she'd never looked better in anything else. Her opinion, then, was of substance; but the real proof was the vision now approaching me.

As we drove to the vineyard that had become our favorite haunt for these outings, she informed me that she couldn't stay late because she had an evening date with Dirk. The freedom that I couldn't deny her made her soar in exultation, but the realization that the dress was meant for someone else's eyes filled mine with stinging tears of pain as I struggled to maintain composure. She noticed and tried to engage me in small talk, but I kept it even smaller, to monosyllables, convinced that my voice would crack if I uttered so much as a full sentence.

By the time we arrived I had put things in perspective, aware of the relative advantage, if I wanted her, of accepting these occasional disappointments as the price of winning her back, rather than throwing away any possibility of doing so by standing "on principle" and whining about her insensitivity. As we sat down with a bottle of the fruity white wine we always bought there, and a wedge of cheese that we brought ourselves because the vintner had once chintzed out on us, I was back to a reasonably cheery disposition.

"So what's the occasion?" I asked, feigning insouciance. "Mother's Day. He's taking me out for dinner." "Isn't Mother's Day tomorrow?" I asked. I had forgotten all about it. "Yes, but he's spending all day with his mother and he wanted to do something for me, too." I thought to say that the sentiment would be more fitting toward his girlfriend, but of course I refrained. "I don't think we'll be very late," she added, "because he has to drive to North Carolina in the morning. I'll call you if I get back early." My color must have rushed back, because she was grinning.

A leafy offshoot from an overhanging maple branch kept getting in my face, pushed by the balmy spring breeze. "Move your chair," said Marcela, but I liked where I was sitting so I broke off the annoying branchlet and threw it between the wine shed and an old barn: "There! That'll teach you manners." They laughed at the secondary limb amputation; drastic, Gordian-knot solutions to such minor inconveniences entertained them and gave our time together a zesty, lighthearted tone.

Marcela was adept at such banter. I openly regarded her my favorite stepdaughter because of a keen alertness and sagacity that made her more like her mother than Verónica, I thought, but in fact placed her in a category apart from both of them, as she always picked up on subtle ironies that the others missed altogether. Dirk was picking Silvia up at eight, so at six-thirty I suggested we head back in time for her to get ready for her date. With a darting glance, she scanned me for any sign of sarcasm, but I was playing it straight: I was cool.

I dropped them off and went home. I was about to turn in, but the phone rang at ten thirty. "Are you doing anything?" Silvia asked. "Wow, that was quick!" I noted, with studied objectivity. "It was boring," she said. "He kept talking about his family. I reminded him he had to hit the road early. How about a beer?" I picked her up in ten minutes. She wanted to dance, so we went to Snookers, a pool hall that had a DJ on weekends. We'd gone dancing there before. The music was bad, but there was a lesbian couple practically having sex on the dance floor.

Silvia had often told me that lesbian scenes aroused her—not that she'd ever do that herself (she'd probed me once, though, about a threesome with her friend Adriana). We sat in a horseshoe-shaped booth that blocked her view of the dirty-dancing lesbians, so she leaned far forward to watch them, supporting herself with her hands on the table, her pert derrière emerging slyly from under the LBD. I put my left hand into her, sliding my two upper fingers back and forth along her cunt, whose copious moisture eased my thumb's way into her anus.

In the relative seclusion of the booth, as couples danced and waitresses occasionally walked by, I started tugging at her thong, which she helped me remove by lifting one heel and then the other. It was from a Lola Luna set with an underwire push-up half-bra that exposed her naked, erect nipples as they stalked me from just under the décolletage. She locked into position and I was hand-fucking her amorously, oblivious of the people around us, working her ass and vagina simultaneously, wondering if she would scream in public. But the lights came on: they were closing.

Outside, I asked her to come home with me. "Why? What are you going to do to me?" she asked, in a sex- and booze-driven craze. I told her I was going to fuck her like the slut she was, that she was going to pay for all the time we'd wasted, and similar testosterone-laden trash to further loose the libido oozing from her. "Let's get in the car," she purred, and we continued the sex play even though everyone leaving the club was milling around in the parking lot. They were drunk and unruly, and no one seemed to notice the hanky-panky going on in the Subaru.

In her seated position I could no longer reach her ass, but I continued to manipulate her vulva as she unbuttoned my pants and pulled my penis out in the parking lot. She began to lean over to take it into her mouth when a quick double-tap from the horn of a nearby car drew her attention. She snapped upright like a steel spring and threw my cock aside like a hot potato. "Oh, shit! The police," I thought, but it was worse: Verónica and Marcela were parked right next to us, on the right, peering down from the window of the Bolivian lady's van.

"Send them home," I said. "Tell them you'll see them later. What the hell are they doing here, anyway? Did you call them?" An ugly suspicion overtook me as I recalled that Silvia had gone to the ladies' room right at closing. Had she called them to "rescue" her from the lascivious maelstrom she was swirling into?

"No, no, no! I didn't call them," she kept saying. "No, no! I have to go! Goodbye! I'll see you tomorrow!"

"But, Silvia..."

My cry trailed off as she left. All I had to show for the evening was a pair of wet panties in my pocket. And blue balls.

I was also out of gas, so I went to a nearby station to fuel up. As I stood at the pump I saw the van crawl slowly by, at maybe ten, fifteen miles an hour. They had come around another street and were headed home—arguing, presumably, along the way. I was still too numb to make any sense out of all of this, but I turned my phone on and saw that between eleven and one thirty Verónica had called six times. They'd been trying to locate us. Maybe Silvia was telling the truth. Maybe she hadn't called them.

Maybe.

"Happy Mother's Day!" I answered brightly when I saw Silvia's number on my phone the next morning. She wanted to know if I'd drive them into Washington. The Bolivian lady had sent money to her daughter Ashley, who was treating them to lunch at a waterfront seafood restaurant. Sure, I said, still hornier than upset, and glad that the prior evening's weirdness had apparently blown over. It was also a chance to acquaint myself with Ashley, also in the van at Snookers; a very pretty girl, she always lurked quietly in the background whenever I ran into Verónica and Marcela.

Ashley's mom had a Polish boyfriend who lived in Montreal and she would join him there for months at a time. They ran a moderately successful business together and she was sending her daughter regular remittances to cover their share of the household expenses, plus Silvia and the girls had the use of her van. Ashley was too young to drive it so the arrangement gave her two drivers and a surrogate mother with whom she bonded well. She wanted to express her appreciation with a Mother's Day brunch at her favorite seafood place in DC.

The meal was satisfying—all-you-can-eat lobster, shrimp, Alaskan crab legs—and everyone was in good spirits. The previous night's events hadn't had any lasting ill effect, and Ashley was more talkative than I thought she'd be. When the bill came I offered to pay my own plus something extra, totaling about half the check. I handed Ashley the cash, explaining that I'd like to help, but she stared at me in blank bewilderment. "I'm not paying for this," she said, "I thought you were." Silvia frowned, and started counting bills out of her wallet. Something wasn't right.

I drove them around the city for a while, pointing out a few attractions that they hadn't seen yet, but I was vexed. When I dropped them off I asked Silvia to stay behind and demanded an explanation. "If you didn't have enough money you should've just brought it up with me and not involve Ashley," she scolded me, as if I were guilty of a major *faux pas.* "But you said she was treating you," I came back. "I was only obligated to pay my own lunch. Ashley looked at me like I'm a cheapskate, which I'm not, and it bothers me. What the hell is going on?"

"Why should you worry about what other people think of you?" she countered.

"You don't even know Ashley. Why should her opinion matter?"

Precisely because I didn't know her, I was chagrined that I had made such a bad first impression—not counting the night before.

"You should only care about us, making a good impression with us," Silvia fulminated. "If you loved yourself more you wouldn't be so concerned about the opinions of others."

Suddenly, I saw why they call it pop psychology: it keeps popping up in all the wrong places. The real issue was that she had lied to me. She never gave me a straight answer and instead her demeanor turned hostile and deprecatory. Determined to set the record straight, Monday after work I stopped by their apartment, which I'd never entered, to talk to Ashley. Verónica came to the door and told me that Ashley wasn't there, though I was nearly certain that she was. I explained my discomfiture over the day before, that I wanted to clear things up with Ashley. But she was just a girl, Verónica said, and I had no right to disturb her with grown-up issues. I had run into a stone wall.

I left on Verónica's word that she'd explain everything to Ashley, but I was barely out of the parking lot when she called and threatened to report me to the police if I ever came back to "harass" and "intimidate" them. I turned on a dime, marched up the stairs and knocked on the door. "Here I am," I said. "Call the police."

There was a cruiser about a block away, the next street over, and I waved, though of course the police were too far away to see me. "Oh, please, officer, come over and arrest me," I mocked. "Verónica wants me in jail."

I always acted funny when my blood came to a boil. Of all the foul treachery at the hands of this ungrateful brat, the worst so far was this—though I had no idea what was yet to come. Marcela arrived, presumably summoned by the other, and both maintained a steady stream of invective against me—the spitting image of their mother—until Marcela persuaded Verónica that it was no use, that I wasn't afraid of the police, admitting that I'd called their bluff. They stared at me blankly. Smirking at their spent bravado, I turned around and walked away.

I made no effort to contact Silvia after that. Her brazen mendacity quashed my interest in reaching a *modus vivendi* that might allow us to find some use for each other's company. I wrote a letter to the

Bolivian lady, to clarify whatever wild story they must have told her about my dramatic appearance at her door, since according to them it was she who instructed them to call the police. But I had no way of knowing if she'd read it, and indeed I found out later that she never did. Again, Silvia and I were incommunicado—and, again, it didn't last.

I took up bicycle building as a hobby. I was wrapping a handlebar when Silvia knocked at the front door.

"What do you want?" I asked through the outer glass door, still closed. They'd left some cleaning supplies that belonged to someone she had worked for, she said, and asked if she could come in and look for them.

"Why are you here at all?" I demanded. "I told you I don't want to see you again." "Don't talk like that," she pleaded, because Marcela was with her and I wouldn't want to upset her. As usual, she was playing me.

"Get your stuff and leave," I told her gruffly as I opened. "Do you have another beer?" she asked, taking mine from my hand. Of course, there were no cleaning supplies and, of course, I sent Marcela out for more beer, plus crackers, cheese and a summer sausage. We installed ourselves again on our buckets in the Backyard Cantina, as we'd christened our drinking spot. After a while I let my guard down, and the rocky road of our foolhardy love/hate relationship was on another level stretch... until Marcela brought up Lizzie. She wanted to know if the bike I was building was for my daughter.

"No, this one's for Chris," I said, and mentioned that I'd already given Lizzie a store-bought city bike for school.

"I can just see her now, bragging to her friends about the bike daddy bought her," Silvia sneered, completely unprovoked.

"So, I'm supposed to disown my daughter for not being nice to a woman who was going to leave me anyway?" I snapped back, and the fight was on. Before long she was snarling like a Doberman, and Marcela practically had to drag her away.

Nobody could understand how I could put up with such madness. I couldn't explain it, either. My words were clear: *I don't want to see you anymore.* Yet I'd let her back into my life and, sure enough, she'd start insulting and abusing me at the very first chance, real or imagined. And it wasn't even I who prowled the streets of Leesburg looking for strangers to become my bosom buddies, or whatever.

I must have felt, in some self-loathing corner of my soul, that if she couldn't rain foul bile on her wedded husband, who was the poor girl to turn to?

Musical Chairs

I'd been hitting the Four Leaf Clover on odd evenings. I wasn't drinking heavily, but the occasional gin and tonic helped me relax, put my troubles behind me. Sometimes, though, they were sitting right in front of me. Dirk was in a booth one evening, the usual cigar and laptop in front of him, and I approached him, who knows why. "Could we have a word?" I said. Silvia must have told him of my report to her on our previous chat, so he declined with a snort—no more "bro" for me. "Yeah, better not," I concurred. "But you'd better be ready to go the distance, because I am."

I winced instantly at my own mawkish, empty bluster. I walked over to the end of the bar and ordered a drink. Out of the corner of my eye I saw that he switched from one gadget to another, and was tapping furiously away at his BlackBerry. Of course! He was waiting for Silvia, and now he was alerting her to my presence. Sensing fun, I jumped into the fray: "Your boyfriend is here," I texted her in English, "and he's very anxious to see you." She texted back, in broken English: "OK, I go to gym." She was replying to the wrong sender.

I hadn't intended to trip her up, but the confusion was working for me. I couldn't pass up the opportunity for mischief, so I continued impersonating agent Dirk: "What a jerk! He actually thinks you care about him! How could you hook up with such a loser? At least you got a visa out of him. Once you get the divorce, it's gonna be just me and you, Babe!" I thought I was giving myself away by the length of the message (and the reference to the movie pig), but again she texted back: "LOL. I go to gym now. See you soon in gym."

I finished my drink and left the bar, avoiding eye contact with the dangerous undercover operative. Having missed her message, he didn't know what she was doing, but I did, so I installed myself on a sidewalk bench just outside the gym, two doors over from the bar. She showed up within five minutes. Marcela was driving the Bolivian lady's van and offered to stand by when she saw me, to protect mommy. Silvia waved her away and sat beside me on the bench.

"What are you doing here?" she asked.

"Waiting for you," obviously.

My little prank had worked, but it didn't do me any good. I just sat there, doleful and despondent. "Why don't you go over and hang out with your boyfriend?" I moped. "You don't have to hide now." She still wasn't aware of how our rendezvous had come about. "What are you talking about? I'm just here for my spinning class." The lie irritated me further. "You texted me instead of Dirk, and he doesn't know that you're here. He's still waiting at the Four Leaf Clover. Tell him I sent you."

As always, she stuck to her story, even knowing that she was busted: "Listen, Daniel, I can tell that you're upset. You've been through a lot lately and you're not thinking clearly. Go home and I'll call you after spinning class." I said OK and walked over to the Seven Eleven for a pack of cigarettes, but came back to the bar just a few minutes later. She was sitting with Dirk, and I approached them. He coiled up as if to jump me but I stood him down: "This doesn't involve you. I need to say something to Silvia." I crouched down and whispered: "You see? You lied to me. How can I ever believe anything you say?"

As I walked away I could hear her protesting that the class had been cancelled, that she just happened to run into Dirk, that she was only waiting for Marcela to pick her up. Had he known Spanish, Dirk would have also known that she was lying. Silvia knew that too, of course, and took full advantage of it; she probably spun him a different story later. It was amazing how stupid she took me to be—but I really was, for she'd gotten away with her deceptions, not once or twice, but systematically. No wit or cleverness, no insightful introspection could equip me with the fortitude to acknowledge what I deeply wanted to avoid: that she couldn't care less.

And so, I still had hope. No one's blinder than someone who refuses to see, they say in Colombia. Even faced full-strength with proof of Silvia's raw contempt for me, I clung to the conceit that it was a temporary estrangement, with a beginning and an end. When did it start? Why? If I knew the answers I could fix it, I told myself, and bring back the happiness we once had. How could Guantánamo not be true? An entire universe revolved around that moment. She had strayed from a path we had embarked on together, but she'd find her way back—yes, she'd come back!

Besides, I had done my part to drive her away. I had lost my temper and blown up at her. I had promised myself long before that I would root out my explosive anger, for all the hurt it had brought me and others. But I had failed, and lost control when I most needed it. Who could blame Silvia for turning her back on me? And of course she was entitled to some measure of financial responsibility on my part. She had left her family, her country, and needed reassurance from a man who could provide at least a modicum of material security.

My self-deprecation became ruthless and abiding, a full-time occupation. If owning up to my flaws would give me back control of the situation, I'd embrace self-deprecation as a pathway to freedom, even as the chains of illusion continued to shackle my soul. Every effort to extricate myself from the doubts that confused and consumed me created new ones, further feeding my addiction to pain. I began to fear that my mind would turn against me, as it had years before when the black night of depression landed me, heavily sedated, in a hospital bed.

I scoured the Internet for guidance to rebuild my relationship with Silvia. I paid thirty bucks to download a program called Get Your Girl Back, with a fair amount of useful advice—things that I knew, mostly, but could benefit from practicing: "Don't beg, don't chase. Work on yourself, whom you control; not the other person, whom you don't. Become again the man she was first attracted to. Visualize having won her back already, but never assume any attributions that she hasn't given you of her own accord. Define your own commitment clearly."

These, at least for me, trite truisms, did the job of putting me in a more reasonable frame of mind. Above all, the notion that losing her wouldn't be the end of the world, even if I followed every step religiously, slowly pulled me away from the brink. Better yet, it actually began to work. In the absence of the fierce intensity with which I had earlier expected her to requite me, she did, in fact, open up to me again, although her rights and freedoms were always foremost in her mind. I taught myself to accept that, and our contacts grew in frequency.

The toughest part was accepting her "friendship" with Dirk, which I detested, convinced that it had started behind my back when we still lived together. But if I wanted a workable relationship with her in the present, I had to waive any claims against past disloyalties or even infidelities. And she insisted over and over that he was just a friend, that she hadn't had sex with him, and that he truly loved his Filipina girlfriend. His only interest in Silvia was, she swore, as a beer pal and conversation buddy. I simply had to swallow it.

The idea of "friends with benefits" appealed to her. She probed my amenability to such arrangements, but I was unwilling to share such "benefits" with other "friends" and made that very clear. She fancied herself a liberated woman, but her Colombian role models in that respect crossed the line into abject flooziness: they were not honest in their dealings with their multiple partners and hid them from each other while reaping gain from all. I was ever flustered at Silvia's inability to balance freedom and commitment but still, I waited.

Her pragmatism clashed with my romantic credo; both stood in the way of merely convenient arrangements that could have only partially met our divergent goals. She chided me for "moralizing"—ironically, after transgressing so many taboos together —but as far as I was concerned (though I kept it to myself) we were still married, and if she came back, it would be as my wife. Nonetheless, we were seeing each other regularly, and both, I thought, were beginning to savor the relaxed, cunning amity with which our relationship began.

Still no sex, though. My self-help guru more or less held as dogma that the final measure of success in mending a relationship is a return to intimacy, but nothing yet. In our now daily outings I began to hear from Silvia certain indications of dissatisfaction with the orangatoon. I treaded lightly for fear that any crowing might come back to bite me, but I sensed that the easy, open familiarity we had always enjoyed together could easily trump whatever stiff, phony "relationship" Dirk and she could muster across hard cultural and language barriers. It hadn't yet occurred to me that it's easier to lie when the other person *doesn't* speak your language.

I spotted Dirk at the Wellmark parking lot one Sunday, exiting a gray Mercedes-Benz tagged DRMBOAT; he really liked that car, he'd have everybody know. Silvia had once boasted that her friend owned a Mercedes, which made him, axiomatically, a Good Catch. He swaggered across the lot with a droll, pronounced stoop, arms akimbo as if packing heat, further bolstering my hypothesis that he was an ex-fed on contract with Homeland Security. What a find! In one man she could quell her penchant for both hunchbacks and cops. But enough...

Focusing on the requisite self-control prescribed by Get Your Girl Back, I pushed out of my mind all feelings of jealousy and refused to play the victim. I was better than that, I knew, and the truth would out. Accepting her right to see another man on a "Platonic" basis—or maybe more, though she denied it—had drawn her closer to me as a "friend" to laugh with and share moments of whimsy. We'd sometimes shop at a nearby Asian market, and she'd ask me into the house for a beer or two. But still, *no sex!*

I walked her up to her apartment one afternoon when the girls weren't back from work yet. She handed me a beer and went to her room to change. I had a huge erection, thinking it was finally my day, when she emerged wearing a blue evening dress. "Do you like it? Dirk bought it for me." I was appalled. She was showing off her *loot!* To *me!* "He took you shopping?" I asked, not hiding at least some of my shocked disgust. "Yes, at Norstrand." It looked fancy, about $400. "No, it makes you look like an old lady. Maybe if you take off ten, twelve inches."

I couldn't finish my beer and made an excuse to leave. The erection, needless to say, was gone. Maybe she wanted me to fuck her in Dirk's dress, she was so twisted, but I was completely beside myself. The Get Your Girl Back guru was screaming in my ear, telling me to maintain control, but I felt like strangling him. It wasn't even a pretty dress! The entire scene was so impossibly inane that I actually got around to chuckling about it on the way home, and feeling sorry, in fact, for Silvia, whose world had shrunk to such a sad parody of what once we'd had together.

I began to write a letter: "I didn't have much, but you had all of me, not the scraps of attention that a cold, dishonest man throws your way in exchange for company by the hour. You threw away an honest love for the sake of mere convenience and material comfort. That's the kind of cheap, venal thinking that debases your feelings and diminishes your soul. You didn't betray me; you betrayed yourself. You allowed yourself to become a commodity." But I didn't send it. I stuck with Get Your Girl Back.

Letting Go

"If you love somebody, let them go." I took the old saw with a grain of salt, because I had owned a wayward beagle that would disappear all night when I let him off his leash. He'd return, all right, in the morning, exulting in the stench of all the decomposing treasures he'd encountered in his voyage of discovery, that made everyone in the house gag. He was spent from trekking and wanted nothing better than to take an all-day nap, but I had to drag him into the bathroom and wash him thoroughly in the tub, always an intense man-dog bonding experience.

Not that he was disobedient. Over time Rusty became highly responsive to the four-word lexicon I used to tell him what to do, or not to, even though everyone told me that beagles are essentially untrainable. "No" referred to anything he was doing, which he was to cease immediately; "stop" meant in his tracks, usually when he'd arrived at a curb and I had to keep him out of traffic; "go" was permission to cross the street; and "c'mere" meant, "if you come back I'll pat your belly and scratch you behind your ears." It wasn't German, but it worked.

Such obedience vanished, though, as soon as he was out of sight from me, which he inferred from the fact that I was out of sight from him. As long as he could see me, he complied with my commands, but if he couldn't, he pretended he couldn't hear me, either, and figured he was on his own. He would inch gradually toward the limits of my sphere of vision, glancing furtively from time to time to see if I still had an eye on him, and if I didn't, he'd dash blissfully into the wild. When I busted him, he'd give me a soulful look that said, "Who, me?"

Unlike Rusty, Silvia was no dog, and I couldn't impose on her the will of a superior species. Also, she bathed herself, though what reeked about her was her attitude, and that wouldn't come out with soap. In the spirit of radical democracy with which she had politicized our vestigial relationship, I decided to give her what she wanted, even if it meant agreeing with those feel-good e-mails with pretty landscapes and New Age music, and that scathing diatribe against me by her sister Norma, whom I'd never known to say anything true.

I got in touch with Benjamin Steinberg, my lawyer from my first divorce. Ben had seen me through a gruesome custody fight that didn't stop at allegations by my first wife of abuse and neglect of the children, six and four, that she'd unilaterally left me to care for when she stomped out of the house in pursuit of a dream of unrestricted freedom and a man who wasn't all that interested in her, after all, when she tried to move in with him in Miami. Fortunately, Ben instructed me to change the locks, so when she returned she was homeless.

Silvia and I had an eight o'clock appointment at Ben's office and I had posted myself on a sidewalk bench across the street, waiting for her, when Dirk drove by in his baby blue Volkswagen. I gave him a steely glare, dragging fiercely, like Clint Eastwood, on a cigarette that I hadn't, however, rolled myself. The car wasn't right, either; he should have been driving a dusty pick-up truck. When Silvia arrived twenty minutes late, duly flanked by daughters left and right, I asked her why Dirk was cruising the block, and she said she didn't know.

Left daughter Verónica's involuntary downward glance, however, told me that *she* knew. Since learning about Silvia's boyfriend I'd always felt that Verónica was pimping her out to him, covering up for her escapades. I wondered if she might have met him first, but... what about the dictionary? She held something over her mother's head, probably something to do with the story about their father cutting off their tuition. In the midst of a spiteful rant she once said that all I'd ever done for them was pull them out of school, but immediately bit her tongue.

Upon entering the office building we found that Ben no longer worked there, but I called and he was willing to wait for us at his new office in a farmhouse twenty minutes west. "We don't have time," huffed Verónica. "Come on, Ma, let's go. You can do it another day." I asked Silvia if she couldn't speak for herself, if Verónica was her legal guardian. After all, it was *they* who had arrived late. "You see, Ma? He's impossible; you can't talk with him. We have to get to work. Let's go."

Silvia remained speechless, staring helplessly at both of us.

"We do it now, or we don't do it," I put my foot down. I was already missing work and it had been difficult enough to bring myself to accept this, I told Silvia; I wasn't sure I'd have the nerve to go through with it some other time. She agreed, and the girls had to also, because they really didn't have to be there in the first place, and I could take Silvia myself if they were too busy to give her a ride.

"Aren't you going to call Dirk to tell him where you're going?" I asked Verónica, who turned, from livid fury, crimson red.

Verónica insisted on going over the entire nine-page property settlement agreement in Spanish. Since I was the only interpreter in the room, at Ben's suggestion I sight-translated the document as Verónica followed closely on another copy, nodding gravely at each paragraph that she barely understood in either language. When it was time to sign I asked Ben if he had anything to drink, and he poured me a glass from a decanter of excellent single-malt.

"To your freedom," I toasted Silvia as she signed, tearfully, under Verónica's watchful eye.

They hadn't noticed that the main purport of the PSA was to protect my financial interests, while paying lip service to the personal liberties that Silvia had been enjoying anyway. Though there was little I could lose to her in a financial dispute, the agreement reduced my exposure to zero. I was safe, but also sorry. Ben was semi-retired at this point and he joined me for another drink after Silvia and her daughters left. I broke down: "I still love her, man." He put his arm around my shoulders: "If she's really yours, she'll come back."

Aunt Ellie

I wanted sex with Silvia, but that wasn't the reason I wanted her back; I actually loved her. I craved the body I had explored so thoroughly, that she had surrendered so completely to me in pursuit of a sexual freedom that had seemingly run off course. She saw that freedom not as defined by its boundaries, but by an absence thereof—so it was, essentially, undefined: what good is it to do anything you want, if you don't know what that is? She reached for new horizons that became increasingly elusive as she moved away from a point of reference, which should have been her love for me.

That's what *I* thought, anyway.

I started looking for other indicators, engaging her on other levels. This wasn't new with us; it had always occurred naturally, even during sex, and especially afterward, when conversation ranged galactic, often at the very edge of meaning, the nakedness of our bodies a proper setting for the openness of our minds. Once that threshold was crossed, we entered a dream world all our own. Sex was a gateway to a heightened state of empyreal luminescence; her laughter, her rapt exaltation during those voyages beyond space and time, had convinced me that she'd got it.

So I craved her body, that I might own her heart. I had lost her, I thought, because communion of the flesh had dropped below the fifty-one percent mark on her value scale, so she no longer had an anchor and was adrift in a sea of other values than those we shared to the extent we felt they were worth marrying for. Now I was no longer the reason her life had changed, but merely a fading feature in a new landscape that dazzled and confused her as she became increasingly unmoored. She wanted other things. It wasn't her sexuality she was giving up; it was her *reason.*

Addressing the problem "non-sexually," I took a new approach to the relationship by creating opportunities for Silvia to connect to the "spiritual" dimension (we'll call it that) of a love that had been so strong in both of us. I wasn't sure why she kept seeing me, if she wasn't going to fuck me, so I began to explore other avenues to exist again at that deeper level we used to access through sex. When she noticed that I no longer seemed so preoccupied with getting laid, she started calling more assiduously, showing greater interest, and we'd talk about other things.

I asked her to come with me to visit my aunt Elise, who lay prostrated from a massive stroke some three years earlier. Ellie was my mother's only surviving sister in the United States, and when I visited her I'd get mom on the phone from Colombia. The two sisters would engage in lively one-way conversation, at least in the sense of *verbal* content, because my aunt remained highly expressive and responded with appropriate facial demeanor to the emotional tenor of different subjects, which signaled to me that she was, though speechless, fully sentient.

On the way to the nursing home, about two hours away, Silvia went into nostalgic reverie over how good things had once been between us. I tried to steer the conversation into a more useful consideration of where we stood now, and could further stand if the cobwebs that had clouded our judgment could be swept away and the light that had shone so clearly in those better moments could bring our "friendship" once again out of darkness. She couldn't see the darkness, though, because her eyes were closed, and her memories were merely anecdotal, idle chat.

When we arrived, Elise, as usual, came aglow with a smile of overwhelming brightness and showered kisses on my hand, which she held close with her left one, the only one she could move. She had never met Silvia so I introduced her, still as my wife, because there was no point in going into details, and besides we really were still married. She also kissed her copiously, making me wonder, still, if she knew who we were. I wanted to believe that she was of sound mind, but I had no way of gauging her actual cognitive capacity.

The stroke had occurred soon after the death of her husband Stan, a gruff World War II veteran I had visited at the hospital as he died of stomach cancer. "At times like this is when you realize who your real friends are," he told me with a depth of feeling that in him was highly unusual. I would always rue my answer, as I tried to restore levity by joking, "I'm not your friend, Stan; I'm your nephew." I meant no offense, of course, and wanted to rectify my clumsy gaffe the next time I went to see him, but the hospital bed was empty.

He was buried with honors at Quantico National Cemetery, but I was aghast when the Army Honor Guard unit assigned to the ceremony played a recorded "Taps" on a boom box that looked like it had lost its way to a beach party, sitting awkwardly on a chair by the casket. Had they run out of buglers? Fortunately the kids had come along to see Stan off with a little string quartet they put together with a couple of orchestra friends. They played the sweet, elegiac *largo* from Vivaldi's "Winter," deeply moving on this uniquely appropriate, windy occasion.

Aunt Ellie missed the funeral, because she was hospitalized with congestive heart failure. A workaholic, she never gave up on tending to a lush flower garden she'd been growing around the house since Stan had built it in the sixties. She was stubbornly opposed to any allopathic treatment of her condition, preferring home and herbal remedies that she claimed were "healthier." No one knew how long she'd lain unconscious on the floor when they found her after missing church one Sunday. She had sustained catastrophic brain damage.

Mom wasn't picking up the phone in Colombia, so it was just me in the room with Ellie, and Silvia, who engaged her with the stuffed animals that had become her bedside companions, made up little games that delighted her, as if playing peek-a-boo with a baby. Silvia took off the bracelet that Erica, the Jamaican artist, had given her in Miami, and put it on Ellie's wrist, where it still was the next time I went to see her. She showed it to me with an inquisitive look: why hadn't I brought back the pretty girl who had given it to her? On some levels we understood each other very well.

The hardest part about visiting her was always leaving, because she'd clutch my hand and moan dolefully, and I couldn't bear it. I didn't want her to see any trace of sadness on my face, so I asked Silvia to distract her as I snuck away. When Silvia came out of the room I was weeping in the hallway. Reflecting in her eyes my own sorrow, she wrapped her arms around my waist and pressed her cheek against my breast, lifting from my heart a crushing heaviness. She'd never shown me quite such tenderness before. But what was going on with Dirk, then? Still, confusion.

New York

Silvia's friend Pilar, who'd been with us at our wedding, had been staying with a friend in New York for a few weeks. Silvia asked if we could pick her up and bring her to Leesburg for a quick visit, and if she could stay at my place for a while, because they were hesitant to receive guests at their apartment. The Bolivian lady was still in Canada, but they expected her back any day. My years in New York had been among my fondest and I'd described the vibrant city in glowing terms to Silvia and her daughters. I looked forward to showing them around.

I had some comp time so I left work early Friday afternoon. Ashley tagged along, which filled the car, and I wondered where Pilar would sit on the way back. We found her at a lugubrious housing project on Second and 91st. A gaggle of Dominicans loitering in the courtyard eyed us curiously but lost interest when they realized that we weren't customers. Pilar burst out the front door and hurried to the car, relieved that her anxious wait was over. She didn't have a phone so we'd been unable to tell her we were running late. She squeezed into the back somehow.

After that initial exposure to the seedy side of Manhattan (don't even *ask* about the South Bronx, I teased them) I drove them down Fifth Avenue and then back up Park to 42nd Street and the mandatory walk through Times Square. "So there you have it," I boasted to Silvia: "New York." The dazzling lights and electronic displays were even gaudier than the last time I'd been there, years before, but I knew that was what they expected, and they were not disappointed. I dropped them off at Broadway and drove around the block to find a parking space.

They were taking pictures of each other on their cell phones when I joined them and undertook to share some insight into the high-powered urban habitat. "New Yorkers have an ill-deserved reputation of being cantankerous and rude," I explained, "but when you get to know them they're actually very nice. That's not going to happen tonight, though, because there probably isn't a single New Yorker in this entire crowd; they're all tourists, like us," I exaggerated, just to give the story a little added punch.

"But wait, here comes the mayor!"

A grungy street person was working his way through the throngs, carrying a huge amount of boxes and bags impossibly fastened together in a shapeless bundle slung over his shoulder, holding that with one hand and a walking stick in the other. He looked like Lucky, from *Waiting for Godot.* "Good evening, sir," I greeted him affably, and was about to introduce my company, but he lunged at me, muttering cusswords and swinging at me with his stick. "We must have caught him at a bad time," I explained, stepping gingerly to remain out of his reach.

The girls were confused, yet refused to believe that the cranky old bum really was the mayor of New York. I couldn't let them leave the Big Apple, even after so short a visit, without at least a taste of its inimitable unpredictability. After all, I had witnessed knife fights on the A train on the way home from a newspaper job at three in the morning, and still remembered the hapless young man, left naked by attackers, who ran screaming into the 42nd Street subway station we were now facing, jumped the turnstile and grabbed the third rail with both hands.

"But why did he do that?" they asked.

"He didn't have any tokens," I explained, but they didn't know what tokens were, so the joke tanked ingloriously. What they really wanted to know was why he'd killed himself.

"Well, wouldn't you?" I asked.

They thought about it as we walked to the car. We were traveling back the same night and I still had a few sights to show them, so we drove crosstown on 34th Street, but the Empire State Building isn't as awesome from up close. St. Patrick's Cathedral, however, is a neo-gothic jewel from any angle.

Skipping quickly through Rockefeller Center (I told them the story about Diego Rivera, and promised to bring them to the skating rink in winter) we came to the Avenue of the Americas, the quintessential expression, for me, of the skyscraper paradigm that New York gave Western Civilization. Evenly spaced and lined up like shrubbery, the buildings, though not the tallest in town, best articulate that change of scale. The stately array of colossal dominos, daring the gods to flip the first one over, always took my breath away. But it was time to go.

I couldn't tell what effect, if any, my guided flash tour had on Silvia, Verónica, Marcela, Ashley and Pilar, but I'd done what

I could, in the limited time available, and had lived again for a moment, in my heart, my old love affair with the city. This much I could share with them: a passion as strong as one might experience with a person deeply cared for. I still longed for Silvia's heart, still hoped to touch it, so I gave her New York.

On the way back Pilar, who was taller than the others, rode with me in the front passenger seat. By the time we emerged from the Lincoln Tunnel Silvia and her three girls were already asleep, bundled snugly together like ferrets in the back. Pilar did her best to engage in conversation, ostensibly to help me stay awake, but halfway down the New Jersey Turnpike she dozed off, too, leaving me alone with my thoughts and a CD of African pop music I was fond of. Dawn was breaking as we dropped off the ferrets and drove home. I let Pilar have my bed.

I made a hearty breakfast of sausage, toast and eggs with onion, cheese and tomato scrambled in, only to find, when I woke her, that Pilar was on a diet. Silvia had a baby-sitting job and her daughters were working, too, so I took Pilar on a walking tour of the historic district, where we found the gravesites of William and Ida Lee Rust, a town notable and his grandmother, after whom the public library and recreation facility behind the cemetery were named. Ida Lee was indeed a relative of the Confederate general, I finally confirmed. In 1902 she'd spoken out against the mob lynching of a black man awaiting trial in the Loudoun jail. No one listened.

Silvia changed her mind about hosting Pilar, so the girls picked her up when they got off work and she remained with them the rest of the week. I talked Jerry Parker into joining us at a salsa club in DC that Friday, but there was zero chemistry between him and Pilar, and Silvia was being a jerk with me, also. Pilar had to get to New York for her flight back to Colombia, so we drove her into Washington on Sunday and she took the bus.

Etilio's

I began to visit more frequently with my friend Etilio, an older Mexican interpreter I knew from my traveling days with the State Department. His parents must have been drunk when they named him, saddling him for life with an association that made him the butt of tiresome alcohol jokes that he shrugged off, nevertheless, with cool forbearance, or sometimes flipped back wryly on the assailant. Although an assiduous social drinker, he was no drunk, and had a formidable capacity for substantive, nightlong conversation about anything at all, like Socrates.

Born in Veracruz, he was almost Cuban, with the attending picaresque, offbeat wit that made it an endless delight to spar with him. He kept mixing drinks from his well-stocked bar, which we referred to affectionately as "Etilio's." I'd call ahead: "Is the bar open?" "Why sure, Danny," he'd invariably reply, "Come on over." His real age was a closely guarded secret, but I guessed, extrapolating from anecdotal references, he was about eighty. He had retired long ago from the Organization of American States, but still freelanced occasionally.

In matters of love, Etilio was a cynic, and at times I felt sorry for him, sure that he was merely masking his loneliness. Then again, though I didn't share it, looking at things from his point of view often uncovered hidden flaws in my own thinking, and instead of pity for him I felt admiration. He wasn't so much against love as against marriage, which he saw as the opposite of love: a toxic bog that always smothers it. Since my marriage to Silvia, at least on one level, was a mere formality to bring us together, he was right.

That was precisely the point: while I wanted her to be in the States because I loved her, she loved me because she wanted to be in the States. What I saw as a means to an end, to her was an end in itself, so the love that brought her to me was no longer needed once she arrived, but for the unexpected delay in bringing up her daughters. It was difficult for me to look at things so coldly, but a few *mojitos* made it easier to swallow the idea.

Etilio never met Silvia, but seemed to know her better than I, and he knew exactly what was going on. Politely, though—ever the diplomat—he never told me straight up what he really thought, stripped of euphemisms. He was even supportive of my lingering relationship with Silvia, though never yielding in his firm conviction that marriage is in every case a lost cause.

When I mentioned that she'd proffered the "friends with benefits" alternative, he said, "Great! That way you can get all the fucking you want, without the fucking over." He had to agree with me, however, that in *her* case I'd still get the latter, the illusion of the former merely dangling as bait.

Yet, ever the optimist—or the fool—I entertained the conceit that I was a tough, wily carp that could capture the bait without swallowing the hook, and continued to play Silvia's game. My job hunt had yielded an interview for an attractive position with the Northern District of California, in San Francisco. I meant to keep the news from Silvia but blurted it out with irrepressible candor one evening over beer at her place. I wasn't quite the carp I fancied, although the bait I now dangled before her made me a kind of fisherman, or a bad excuse for one.

Silvia had always expressed a preference for city life, and was dismayed to find, upon arriving, that Leesburg offered no such thing. There were many things that didn't live up to her high expectations, but San Francisco sounded like a promising twist of fate. I cautioned that a mere interview was, at best, a fifty-fifty chance of actually getting the job and, besides, wasn't she the one who insisted on remaining independent, and was intransigent in demanding a divorce?

"Cast out negative thoughts," she shot back, from her arsenal of pop psychology.

"Ma, if Danny gets that job in San Francisco, maybe we could move there with him," Verónica surprised me by suggesting. She had vehemently opposed Silvia's continuing to see me, and had pandered openly to her dalliance with Dirk. And yet, I pondered the idea: could there still be a basis for a more equitable relationship? The girls would soon be leaving for college or the Armed Forces, and Silvia and I might have a chance of salvaging whatever was good about the marriage before they arrived. But there was no point in speculating yet.

The interview went well, and a few days after my return the San Francisco coordinator called for an in-depth follow-up. We saw eye-to-eye on fundamental aspects of interpreting practice, as her career had also traversed the conference and other venues, giving her a broader outlook than the average court interpreter. Our acquaintance grew into a technical collaboration between our offices, but a month later she called to inform me that the vacancy had been withdrawn due to a federal hiring freeze in that jurisdiction.

"There will be other opportunities," Silvia said coolly when I told her the news. She had said exactly the same thing when the IMF job failed to materialize, although on that occasion she sounded hopeful and supportive, whereas now she was merely shrugging it off, having no stake in the matter. I'd sensed long before that she didn't doubt my abilities; she simply wasn't going to wait around for results as long as she had other options, and she never stopped shopping for those. Disappointed, I gave Etilio a call:

"Is the bar open?"

Atlantic City

Silvia's nephew Rafael, a taciturn thirteen-year-old, came to visit his aunt and cousins. I took them all out a couple of times, and worked overtime to coax from him some sign of life. He was to join his mother Norma in Atlantic City, where she was working at a beauty parlor. No one asked, but I knew what Silvia wanted, so I offered to drive and the trip was on. I was ebullient, even manic, on the way, and broke a hundred on the New Jersey Turnpike, dancing delicately through traffic. For a moment I thought I saw Rafael crack a grin, but maybe he was just passing gas.

We met Norma outside a Dunkin' Donuts. I thought we were driving right back, but Silvia had other plans. Norma took us to her new digs in the attic of another Colombian home. Verónica and Marcela couldn't come, but Ashley had joined us for the trip. She'd become quite attached to Silvia during her mom's extended Canadian sojourns, and clove to her as we took a stroll on the boardwalk. Norma insisted on showing us the casinos, but the hordes of destitute, demented old ladies pouring their social security money into slot machines were an utterly depressing sight. Silvia, for once, agreed.

On the way back we picked up a twelve-pack. I wouldn't be driving so I had a few, though not as many beers as the others, including Ashley, who'd just turned sixteen. She was a high-school hottie used to staying out all night, and could hold her own against all comers; her mom simply misunderstood her, Silvia said. We got hungry and took an outdoor table at an airy Mediterranean café, back on the boardwalk. Ashley ordered a piña colada. Had they carded her, she would have said she meant a *virgin* one (she winks); but they didn't, so she ordered two more.

A gentle ocean breeze and Arabian lounge music ramped up the *joie de vivre,* although Rafael wasn't happy with his mom's nagging about the "right" way to eat linguine. I suggested that he just enjoy the food, but he wasn't drinking, so he was uptight. And taciturn. After dinner Silvia pulled me back as the others walked home. We leaned against the railing and I squeezed her ass against my cock, that leapt for joy at the chance to rub against her. "So what are you thinking?" she asked. "That I'm liking this a lot," I burbled. "Doing anything tonight?"

The others were a block ahead and Ashley turned back occasionally, stumbling slightly, but Norma herded her on. When they turned off at her street we lingered further on the beach, kissing, fondling. As we came upstairs they were settling down on improvised mats of folded bedspreads. Silvia took the bed, Ashley sprawled out right beside it, and Rafael bedded down by his mother across the room. I felt awkward asking where to sleep, because I still had no rights, express or implied; but Silvia patted the empty space beside her: "Lie down here awhile."

The lights went out with the dying embers of conversation, rambling, drowsy thoughts trailing off mid-sentence. I could smell the ocean on her skin as she arched her back so that I could reach inside her unzipped shorts. I managed to slip two fingers into her cleft and struggled awkwardly to pleasure her. I gave up and rolled away, but she grabbed my hand and pulled it back. "Don't stop," she whispered. "I'm going to come."

"But I can't reach down there, it's..."

"Shhh. I'll be right back." She went to the bathroom, stepping lightly, but stumbled slightly over Ashley in the pitch black of the windowless room. I removed my pants.

When she returned she was wearing an oversize T-shirt she had brought for the beach. She lay again beside me and I reached below: no panties. As I began to finger her again she separated her legs and looked fiercely into my eyes, the bright black gleam of hers piercing the darkness, jet fire burning from within.

"You cannot tell anyone," she whispered hoarsely, and I said OK.

"Promise me." OK.

"Promise me..." I covered her mouth with mine and took her breath away. The rhythm was building.

Her hips began to rock and she could barely keep from waking everybody up— though I had my doubts that Ashley, lying next to us, was actually asleep. She came quickly, suppressing her convulsive spasms, and grabbed ferociously for my penis. I let her play with it for a while, but I'd be damned if I was going to settle for a hand job. I turned her on her left side and she drew her right leg up toward her chest, like the last time I fucked her on my first trip to Bogotá—yet she felt tighter, hotter than I remembered as I sank into her silky passage in one decisive, irrevocable thrust.

She gasped, and the bed creaked. They must have heard us, but I couldn't care less. I was wrong about the ocean fragrance; it was her vagina, drenched and superheated, its nectar scent now darker, stronger. Charged with anticipation, I ejaculated in a long, pulsing stream that seemed to originate in the back of my brain and dragged along the entirety of my existence, momentarily immortal. I stayed inside her as we dozed off, fire quenched, my right thigh on her left one, in overlapping fours. Sweet, warm tears welled up behind my closed eyelids. I had made it. I was home.

In the morning, as we stirred, I slung my arm over her shoulder, but she pushed away and ran to the bathroom. When the light came on Ashley was wearing Silvia's T-shirt, I noted. "No, it's *my* T-shirt!" she corrected me, laughing, as amused as I was confused. They wanted to go to the beach. I took a quick shower and went downstairs, chatting briefly with the Colombian family on my way through the living room. I sat on the stoop to smoke a cigarette, watching people passing by, and Rafael came out to join me, no longer quite so taciturn—though still somewhat morose.

The girls were taking a while, and I entertained Rafael with talk about cars and motorcycles, surprising him with my knowledge thereof. "Let's go for a ride, kid. I'd like to take a look around." He eyed me oddly, as if wanting to say something but couldn't bring himself to do it. I bought a fresh pack of cigarettes at a Colombian supermarket. The cashier was from Cali, and we talked about salsa. I always hit it off well with *Caleñas.*

When we got back the girls were waiting outside. Norma gave her son a quizzical look, wondering, no doubt, what we'd talked about... but we hadn't. We drove to the beach, parked and set up camp on the gray sand. Silvia wore a zebra-print bikini; Ashley, identically sized but for a smaller bust, borrowed a tiny turquoise one I'd given Silvia years before. It brought out the red overtones of her rich cinnamon skin, but also flattered Ashley's, which was two shades darker. She was clingier than usual with Silvia, possibly sore because I'd fucked her the night before.

Rafael made a fuss about wearing proper beach shoes, so Norma took him shopping for a pair. Ashley let her fingers slide through mine as she left me her camera to go splashing in the waves with Silvia. Her top kept slipping off her coffee-colored nipples, that the cold Atlantic water made rock-hard. She'd laugh and linger a bit before covering back up, playing Lolita to the camera. I myself went briefly Humbert Humbert at the sight of her nubile, firm tush bobbing gaily in and out of the swirling ocean foam. And there was something about her smile...

I was baffled by Silvia's distant, aloof demeanor after our carnal reacquaintance. Maybe it was her period; I'd noticed traces of red dripping off my penis as I showered in the morning. We dropped off Norma and Rafael and hit the road back to Leesburg. I steered clear of any claims or expectations born of the cosmic conflagration still smoldering in my loins. Ashley fell asleep in the back, pouty, bare brown vulva parted slightly, smiling brightly through sheer string panties, legs wide open, pushing tightly against the denim micro-mini she'd slipped into after the beach. Silvia's pubis, too, was shaved, I recalled. It's the new thing.

The days that followed were unnerving, because I had no idea where we stood. I didn't press for an answer, but Silvia's attitude said it all: she had little time for me and, although I was excited about fucking her once more, that didn't seem to mean much to her. The self-help guides all left off where the estranged lovers finally "make out" again, but we'd been there and I didn't feel much better off. My intimate desire was to win back a *wife*, but I wouldn't put it to her quite so. I would have settled for a cozy love affair, but we didn't have that either.

There were so many details that didn't make sense, and I tried to assemble a rationale that could explain them. Why did she want to hide our encounters from her daughters? Why did she push away the morning after, in Atlantic City? She used to be so passionate, but the erotic tension wasn't there. Hadn't we just turned that around, though? What if the distaste she now claimed to feel for Dirk merely masked some other reason she had stopped seeing him? Was it the other way around? My doubts brought me weariness and discontent.

Late from work one day I felt like a drink, so I headed over to the Four Leaf Clover. There they were, seated at the bar, their backs to the entrance. The hopes rekindled in Atlantic City turned to rage at the sight of Silvia consorting again with the aging horse thief whose leg her hand was resting on. Steeling myself for conflict, I approached them from behind and put my arms over both their shoulders. Affecting sympathy in the snidest tone I could muster, I said, "Gee, Dirk, too bad about Silvia's divorce. If she hadn't fucked me last week it could've been final by now."

They turned around to face me. "Now you're going to have to wait another whole year to steal my wife," I continued, removing my arms in case things got physical. "He's just a friend," she protested, pushing him down on his stool so he couldn't get up. "And you're just a slut, a liar and a snake," I replied in Spanish, so that she'd understand me clearly, and her boyfriend not at all. He hadn't yet recovered from his surprise as I further spat: "Either she's cuckolding me with you, or she's cuckolding you with me. One way or the other, she's a tramp."

He decided to cop the hackneyed self-righteousness he'd used on me before: "You better leave us alone, buddy. We're just having a good time. You're harassing us." Fucking nipple-pinching, impotent Nazi. I shot back: "If cheating on your girlfriend and scavenging for other people's wives is your idea of a good time, you must be right." He turned to Doug, the bartender, who'd noticed the commotion. "This is the ex," he said, "and he's harassing us." I interjected: "Well, if you don't feel like chatting, I guess I'll just sit down and have a drink."

I took the stool next to his, on the other side from Silvia, but he wasn't appeased. "You can't sit there," he said. "I always sit here, Dirk. Did you buy the bar now, too?" Again he demanded that Doug do something, but it wasn't working. "You're... a very foolish man," he mustered, straining to keep his composure. "Oh, that really hurts, Dirk," I replied, remaining on the offensive. He finally snapped and said, "I could knock your fucking head off." It was a hiss. "And you have just the training to do that, don't you?" I taunted. "YEAAAHH!" he roared, rising.

"Come on, Dan, sit somewhere else, could you?" Doug entreated me, concerned that a fight would break out. "OK, fine. That shit stinks, anyway," I said, pointing to Dirk's foul stogie. I moved to another stool, around the corner from the disgusting sight of the two-timing lovebirds. As I stepped away I footnoted, "You know, fucking my wife doesn't make you my bro, *bro,*" recycling the patronizing term with which he'd brushed me off months earlier. He glared at me, the closest thing to an expression on his lifeless, empty mug, but stayed put.

"What'll it be, Dan?" Doug asked, remaining cordial although I'd obviously put him on the spot. "The usual," and he brought me a gin and tonic. As he put it down I said, "She's not my ex *yet,* goddammit!" "Cool it, Dan, it's not worth it," he counseled, and of course he was right. The two sat motionless, not a word between them, their eyes glued to a golf game on the screen behind the bar. Surely they would leave, I thought, having rained so heavily on their parade. But they stood their ground, stoically, so I drank up and decided to leave myself.

On the way out I inserted myself again between them, and told Silvia, in Spanish, "I'm going to get this motherfucker to hit me so they'll lock him up." "NOOO!" she cried, springing up to get between us, but I was already in his face: "You know, Dirk, I've never been beat up before. That should be an interesting experience. Why don't we get back to that?" He backed down and said that wasn't really what he meant. "So you're going to hurt me some other way, maybe ruin my life like you guys do to people?" I was reminded of J. Edgar Hoover's treatment of "public enemies."

"Dan, you're nothing but a sorry loser," he sneered. "You couldn't even come up with four hundred dollars for the divorce." Silvia had lied to him about the lawyer's fees; besides, if her divorce was important to him, why not pay for it himself? I sidestepped the issue: "You just don't get it, do you, Dirk? It's not about money. Divorce cannot be granted until a full year has passed since our last 'cohabitation,' and it's only been"—I made a counting motion with my fingers—"oh, eight, nine days." "You're a chronic liar," he said, obviously meaning pathological. "A swine."

Winners and losers. For Dirk, that's what it all boiled down to: the American Way. And the good guy always wins—by definition, because winning *makes* you good. Like a vulture over a dying animal, he was picking the eyes out of our foundering marriage before it was quite carrion. "You guys aren't even living together anymore," he justified his interloping. "But we're still fucking," I clarified, as if such news could rattle this unprincipled opportunist. He was immune: he was carrying the ball, so he was winning, and I was wasting my breath.

Suddenly it struck me what a senseless fix I was in, drawn by a two-bit floozy into a tawdry confrontation with a sleazy scumbag in a bar. I turned and left, not saying another word. I was rid of her at last, I thought, and so would he be, unless he really believed I was lying, in which case he was even dumber than I thought. It didn't matter one way or another, I kept telling myself as I drove home, a blinding succession of conflicting thoughts and feelings racing through my mind. I went straight to my room, shut the door and sobbed bitterly, till sweet sleep came to my rescue.

By calling Silvia on her devious ways, I reflected over the following days, I'd actually done Dirk a good turn—an abhorrent notion but possibly worth it if it denied her the profit of her cold-blooded treachery. I had unspent ammunition with which to further convince him of her deceit, and wrote it down: "Ask her about the time we went to Baltimore in your car (a little buzzy, by the way, and underpowered)—we had a great time. Or when we got drunk at Snookers after her Mother's Day dinner with you. She's lying to you, Dirk, just like she lied to me, and there'll be others after she's done with us."

I doubted, though, that this would shock him, as he seemed to share with her an utter disregard for boundaries of any kind. I kept the piece of paper for a while, thinking to slip it under his windshield wiper, but the idea wore thin: questioning my own motives, I realized that I'd be perpetuating a petty ugliness that by then I just needed to remove myself from. I had already decided to throw it away when I saw them again at the Four Leaf Clover, in the same spot. She saw me but he didn't. I shook my head in disbelief and decided, fuck it, I'll do it. I turned around, found his car outside, and did.

Rug Rash

The truth is, I still wanted her back. As much as I wanted to believe that I'd acted out of a sense of just retribution, I was merely trying to break them up so that she'd come back to me. She was a bitch, I knew, but *my* bitch. In spite of her duplicity, I felt she could love me again as I thought she'd loved me, as she'd *wanted* me before. I saw the girls a couple of times driving the Bolivian lady's beat-up van, and assumed Dirk had stopped lending them the Beedl. Good. The material benefits of their disloyalty gone, the way was clear for me to resume my earlier role.

I texted Silvia and asked how she was doing. "Licking my wounds," she replied. "How about you?" Our earlier familiarity began to reemerge from these timid approaches. At one point she asked me, still by text, how to say something in English. "Why don't you ask Dirk?" I answered. "Surely he's at least as good a linguist as I am." She overlooked the dirty double entendre. "Thanks to you, I can't ask him anything anymore," she wrote. "He won't talk to me." Here we go, I thought: "How about breakfast?" She texted back, "Pick me up in half an hour."

We skipped breakfast and went straight to my place. I had to move because my landlady lost the house in the subprime mortgage crisis. Silvia offered to help and we started putting things in boxes. I'd already moved the bed out and the empty room reminded me of Bertolucci's *Last Tango in Paris.* I wrapped my arms around her from behind. "Let's dance," I said, and she had that grin again: "Do me." She fell to the floor and our clothes flew off. I devoured her with the hunger of our best times together; when she came she let out a loud cry like I'd never heard from her before.

"See? I told you you're a screamer," I teased her, wiping her geyser spray off my face.

"Shut up and fuck me, you bastard," she growled, still writhing, legs spread wide over the steamy dampness of the rug between them—such a tiny cunt, and yet so powerful. I pounded her until my knees bled from rubbing on the carpet. "I love you, Silvia," I blurted out in orgasmic paroxysm as I tumbled to her side. "Do you think we should repaint the ceiling?" she asked, and we belly-laughed at the old joke. I began to think of her again as a partner, and that undead tenderness crept back into my heart. I took her to her place and she told her daughters she was helping me move.

The week that followed was indeed a moving experience. Verónica and Marcela came and went about their business, in my car, and we jumped at every opportunity for sex. I was waiting on news from a new job prospect, so instead of renting another house or apartment I took a room with a Honduran woman that I met through someone at work, with the idea of camping out there until I knew which way my life was going. Lizzie was already in college full-time, and Chris had just a few more months of high school before he would cut loose, too.

One of the little details I missed about living with Silvia was her plasticity of facial expression, which became the subject of a guessing game I used to play with her. Her nose would go from being straight, at rest, to slightly upturned, with a subtle mid-ridge wrinkle, when she was happy, or a drawn-down tip that betrayed distress even if she tried to hide it. Her eyes would also take a distinctly oblique set during sexual rapture, and I called her my "geisha girl," a nickname she liked. I cherished that playful intimacy, and wanted it back.

She came to visit at my new room and wanted to see some erotica I had on my hard drive. We'd been at a cozy little bistro she liked, and she was wearing a flirty outfit with a ruffled, short skirt and a loose-fitting top. As her breathing thickened watching sex scenes, I reached into the top and caressed her turgid nipples and areolae. She brought her legs up, one by one, out of her panties, an Alina Vacariu number with red Zwarovski accents, then rose from the computer and rested her knees on the edge of the bed, a little more than shoulder-width apart.

The skirt brushed against my belly as my cock disappeared up her nether hollow, a little more of it with each groaning shove. "I'm such a slut," she gasped, savoring the reckless abandon she felt by saying so. "You always make me feel this way." Though half-mad with the exquisite constriction of her sphincter, I inquired, "But *whose* slut?" Even in full heat, she was cagey: "Just fuck me, Daniel, fuck my ass. Fill me up," she ordered, "*con esa cosa deliciosa.*"

I rammed her forcefully, driving from my mind, as I tossed her, the distracting thought that she might have said the same thing to Dirk, and he wouldn't have understood her.

No Sense

As I settled in, I began to like my "bachelor's pad" more and more. Silvia still didn't have a license, so I helped her with errands and we'd catch up on sex while her daughters were at work. Things seemed to be working, but it bothered me that she would cut our lovemaking short, insisting that she had to be home before the girls returned. I wasn't

supposed to tell anyone about our "affair" —
though we were still married—and she clung
to the preposterous notion that her daughters
thought we were "just friends." I began to feel
again that queasy sense of foul play.

She had to get her driver's license, I
insisted, so I took her to the Division of Motor
Vehicles. She'd failed the written test three
times already, and couldn't understand how
that could be, having practically memorized
the handbook. Don't think of the test as a set
of questions and answers, I told her, but put
yourself in the driver's seat, visualize each
situation and decide how to deal with it in the
real world. The test was multiple-choice; all
she had to do was then select the answer that
most closely resembled the decision she had
taken "at the wheel."

She was nervous when they called her,
and took forever to finish the test. She came
away from the computer station looking
dumbfounded, so I feared the worst when I
asked her how it went. "I passed!" she said,
hardly believing it. I was genuinely proud,
excited by this seemingly small but, for her,
landmark achievement. I hugged and kissed
her gleefully, effusively, to the amusement of
people sitting nearby. My jaw dropped with

what she said next: "Now I'll be able to drive Dirk's car myself."

I fumed and sputtered. I nearly blew a gasket. I went outside, with a mind to just leave her there, but she still needed the car for the driving test. She came to fetch me, asked me to sit with her inside, but I said I'd better not because I was too angry. The examiner walked her to the car, and when he asked her to switch the high beams on she started the windshield wipers, then the washers, then the hazard lights, etc. "Please be sure she knows what she's doing before you bring her back, sir," he warned me. "She could be dangerous."

They gave her a thirty-day permit so that she could take the driving portion again, but I never took her back, or found out if she'd done it. She blamed me, of course, claiming that my angry outburst had stunned her witless, but I kept my mouth clamped shut as I drove her back to her apartment. She got out of the car, not even thinking to apologize, and I drove away without a word as soon as she shut the door. "That was the last time you'll ever rub that asshole's name in my face," I texted her later. "I don't want to ever see you or hear from you again."

It *still* wasn't true, however, and most certainly she knew it. We reconciled temporarily around the time I was invited to Albuquerque for another job interview, and I asked her to come along. Yet another opportunity to spend some time alone together, I thought, away from the daughters she was so eager to persuade of our non-relationship. She didn't seem to grasp that a three-day trip with me halfway across the country couldn't mean anything Platonic. The interview went well, and we spent the rest of the time sightseeing and making love.

It was a tenuous truce, though. It was as if her body kept sneaking under my sheets against her better judgment—and mine. She asked me to take her to the airport once at dawn. The Bolivian lady was off to Canada again and the girls couldn't give her a ride, so Silvia offered *my* services. There was a two-hour window before work and I didn't want to cut into it driving to her place and back just to drop her off. I needed the rest, so I invited her to take a quick nap with me. But when she came to my side she'd taken her jeans off, and I didn't get any rest at all.

Her skills were sharper than ever, yet she was distant, and wouldn't stay over. She'd look at her watch and claim some reason to get away, usually that her daughters would soon be home, as if that explained everything. "Just tell them we're out picking flowers, like we were in Albuquerque," I'd joke. She was preoccupied. Our trysts were frequent but unpredictable, always with that air of secrecy, and only when *she* wanted it. "What have you done for me to reward you?" she once replied to an urgent booty call. For a "fuck-buddy," she wasn't being much of a buddy at all.

Silvia was planning to spend the holidays in Colombia, and asked me to look after Verónica and Marcela while she was away. They were both adults so the request seemed overwrought, but I agreed. Marcela and I dropped her off at the airport, so loaded with Christmas gifts that we had to unpack her bags, redistribute the weight, and leave things behind in order to meet regulations. An electric guitar she'd ordered for her nephew barely made it in time for us to pick it up at the post office, so she slung it over her shoulder. "I'm a rock star," she tittered.

The girls kept saying that they wanted to spend Christmas with me, as opposed to some other option they seemed not to look forward to. But I was spending Christmas with my children—Chris had moved in with his mom and Lizzie only visited occasionally; I wanted to make every minute with them count —so I promised Verónica and Marcela New Year's Eve. I took them shopping and got them winter wear—nothing fancy because I was rather broke, but their motherless Christmas was acceptably warm and familial.

They'd heard much about the New Year's Eve party at Clyde's, so I took them there. I had lamb shank, Verónica had filet mignon, and Marcela ordered lobster. It was a pleasant surprise to see how happy they were, and especially to hear Verónica, who always had critical comment about everything everywhere, rave about her "perfect" steak. Staff handed out hats and whistles, the girls took pictures on their cell phones, and as the celebration reached a pitched crescendo they called Colombia. We counted down to midnight with their mom on the line. I felt a sense of accomplishment for orchestrating such a memorable family moment.

But when Silvia got back it took her a week to get in touch with me, and then only to ask me to stop by for my Christmas gifts. Certain folksy food items like Tolima tamales and pork roast were now offered in travel-friendly cans, and she also brought trousers and shirts, but I could tell they were from Isabel, whose distinct taste I recognized from previous gifts. "Oh, yes," Silvia confirmed. "I forgot. Isabel sent you those." While she was away, it had been nearly impossible to reach her on the phone. "Can't talk right now," she'd say when she picked up, rarely.

I could smell a rat, but couldn't find it. I was sure that the girls' insistence on being with me over the holidays had something to do with someone else not knowing where they were. They were probably supposed to be with Silvia, in Colombia, but couldn't afford to miss work and needed to hide that from somebody. Whatever deep, dark and probably dumb secret they were keeping, it was just too convoluted, Byzantine, to concern myself with it. My expectations, damped by skepticism, no longer included hearing the truth from them.

Mata Hari

Silvia fancied herself a spy, a mistress of intrigue. She took pleasure in knowing things that she wasn't supposed to know, and would hide from me her means of finding out, pretending to be some sort of seer with supernatural powers, as when she told me her "I can see dead people" stories. Several times while we lived together she had confronted me with matters I had discussed in private with others, as if to show me up as a hypocrite, and that she'd always catch me if I lied to her. She'd challenge me on things I had no idea how she knew.

I'd once asked Lizzie if she'd noticed any improvements in the house since Silvia's arrival, and she answered curtly that it was cleaner. For me, at least, that was something: an acknowledgment, if niggardly, that her father's marriage wasn't a complete washout. But for Silvia it was proof that Lizzie saw her as a lowly maid, and she berated me for countenancing that attitude. I vaguely recalled some such conversation with my daughter, and was pretty sure that it had happened away from Silvia, but Silvia insisted that she'd overheard it from the next room.

What she left out, of course, was how earnestly I had entreated Lizzie to try to understand her, to give her a chance, if not for Silvia's own sake, for me, because she was my wife and I loved her. Did Silvia not hear that part, or was her English comprehension conveniently selective? Months later, however, after she left, she confronted me with proof positive that I had never loved her, because I tried to get in touch with a romantic interest I once had in Venezuela, soon after Silvia moved out of the house. That was true, but there was a twist... a big one.

Karima Zadeh was an exceedingly rare Venezuelan beauty of Moroccan descent and held a successful position in a large financial institution in Caracas. She was a single mother, disillusioned with love. I had met her the same way I'd met Silvia, and around the same time, but our exchanges were more of a literary nature, as Karima wrote very well, and extensively, on a wide range of topics —among them, the short shrift men gave her intellect on account of the sheer physicality of her presence. She was fond of my verse, and I wrote her erotic poems.

"Most men are too stupid to appreciate women smarter than they are," I humored her, "and they get back at them by trying to make them sex slaves." Karima's libido was, in fact, quite healthy, so she wasn't so much against sex as against the power games people play with it, and had become something of a feminist. Yet our conversations were deliciously kinky and we fantasized about meeting in Paris, where I'd fuck her ass on a balcony with a view of the Eiffel Tower—a fantasy I'd lived out with Silvia in Cancún, but overlooking a Mexican gunboat.

Karima was married to her job, and had no interest in becoming anybody's steady girl, much less if it involved moving to the U.S., so I steered my attention to Silvia and eventually focused all of my efforts on her. "But you gave that woman a vibrator," Silvia protested. Yes: a Hitachi HV-250R, just like Simón. And then it hit me: I had mentioned the vibrator when I asked another *Caraqueña,* an architect friend of mine, to help me locate Karima, who had vanished in thin air. And my conversation with Lizzie *had* been private. Both exchanges were *by e-mail.*

"You stole my fucking password!" I realized, and Silvia grinned maliciously, as if she'd beat me at chess. But Víctor had beat her before, when he caught her gleeping his PIN. Maybe it was *Dirk* who hacked me. Silvia relished such invasions of privacy, and gloated over the fact that Dirk had once talked to her about past political associations of mine, which he could only have gleaned from FBI files. I thought of finding out for sure by filing an inquiry under the Freedom of

Information Act, just to mess with him, but it was too much trouble, so I let it go.

I changed the password, and our trysts continued, but they were even more erratic and noncommittal than before, and Silvia was even more insistent on keeping them secret. Though her appetite was healthy, she wouldn't have anything to do with me between meals, and as soon as she was done she was out the door. "Leave the money on the night table," I told her once, half-joking, but she wasn't amused. I objected, but it was a take-it-or-leave-it deal, and all the terms were at her discretion. The sex was pithy, robust, so I figured, "OK, I'll take it."

She would call from time to time, usually asking for small favors. She began to preface her requests with "sorry to bother," "would you mind," and other polite, little acknowledgments that the things I did for her came at a cost to me in time, effort or money—she'd never done that before. While coming across as being more respectful, what was happening was that she was giving herself more personal space, creating a new emotional distance. I read into it that the relationship, for whatever it was worth, was changing course again.

Verónica and Marcela were still using my car regularly, as their friendship with the Bolivian lady had begun to sour. They'd drop me off at work, as before, and keep the car during the day, but a Wellmark coworker gave them a good price on a used convertible one day, and I never heard from them again. I would spot them at times driving around town, the top always down, sporting baseball caps, elbows jutting out the windowsills like movie stars. I was happy for them, in a way, but resented that they no longer had any use for me. I had become irrelevant.

Fully Empty

The last time we made love Silvia resumed her hungry quest for anal fulfillment, stealthy as she lowered herself, well lubricated this time, on my unsuspecting penis. For an excruciating eternity the only part of her body touching mine was the quivering lock ring with which she trapped me in her feverish void, defying gravity—she was *dancing.* She picked up the pace in a steady crescendo, with an explosive internal finale, exulting triumphantly as she drained the life out of her vanquished prey. She had *so* fucked me.

She came to join me in the shower —something she rarely did—soaking up the lubricious pressure of my soapy hands hefting her breasts, of my cock parting her buttocks. "I want your cock," she said, open wide on the bed again as I dried myself. "That may have to wait a bit," I replied, having come so recently. But she was stroking herself with such ardor and finesse, her ring and middle fingers alternately circling her clitoris and plunging down and inward, as we'd often rehearsed over the phone, that my erection returned instantly, with a vengeance.

I took her as I had the first time, unaware that this one was the last. Sometimes there's simply no substitute for the tried-and-true "missionary" position: straight to the heart of the matter. She was surprised— maybe dismayed—that I came again so quickly. Nonetheless I indulged her at length, orally, *post* ejaculation—a reversal of our usual practice— till I was quite sure, from her bucking pelvic spasms and quick, short gasps as the tremors of residual orgasms subsided, that she was done. Then she looked at her watch: "Gotta go. The girls will be back any minute."

How I *hated* that! I lived for the intimate pleasantries we used to enjoy after sex, or as *part* of sex, actually; the most important one, perhaps. Maybe Kundera's *Unbearable Lightness of Being* or Godard's *Breathless* had warped my early sexual development, or I just expected too much. Whatever it was, I wasn't getting it from Silvia; in fact, she *avoided* precisely that. The ennui was becoming unbearable, our conversations increasingly meaningless. She kept putting me off, changing the subject, until I finally snapped, ironically, over a poem.

I traded occasional poems with a Cuban friend in Miami. He'd composed a clever one for International Women's Day, conflating the meaning of the Spanish words for "compelled to absolute passion" and "absolutely impossible to comprehend." I called to share it with Silvia, but when I was done reading she was away from the phone. "Hello? Hello? Silvia?" I kept saying, feeling like a boob. She got back: "Right, you were saying..." For some reason, I lost it just then. "Yes, what *was* I saying, Silvia? How long have I been talking to myself?"

She began to shrug it off: "Well, you know that I'm always doing more than one thing at a time." Indeed. "No, Silvia, not anymore. I'm tired of you taking me for granted, always slighting and dismissing me. I'm not talking to you anymore." I hung up. It was simple, even sophomoric, but I felt a sense of finality: I just wouldn't talk to her anymore! I texted: "I've never been able to count on you for anything. From now on, don't count on me for anything, either."

She was flippant: "LOL! That rhymes!" *Of course* "anything" rhymes with "anything." And "LOL" doesn't mean anything in Spanish.

"You know what, Silvia? I don't want to be your 'friend,' or talk to you, or see you, or know anything about you or your life ever again. I've had it with your games, your lies, your constant disrespect. All you do is piss me off every time we talk or see each other, and it's making me sick. Go ahead and park your ass on some corner and start trolling for *gringo* sleazeballs passing by, because that's about what you rate. I don't give a shit anymore." Our epic romance, you might say, was gone with the wind.

She tried to come back, as usual, by going on the offensive. I had mistaken the time and person of my address, she said: this was 2011, not 1997, and she was Silvia, not my first wife. I dug in deeper and brought up a drunken rage during which she had cast aspersions of incest on me. It was *she* who was confusing time and person, I countered, because Sergio, not I, had committed such transgressions, and possibly worse—was *that* why she was so warped? Good thing I never knew, too, because I wouldn't have proposed marriage, but exorcism.

That finally did it. I held on to my anger as a suit of armor against any new advances, but she never tried to contact me again. Whenever her memory crept up on me I cursed it and kept lashing at it with the vilest, most loathsome associations I had stored in my treasure trove of pain. I worried that the bitterness and contempt I was using to strengthen my resolve could define my character, and I didn't want to become such a creature of darkness. But eventually the hate subsided and I began to enjoy the satisfaction of a job well done.

When I opened my e-mail one day I was surprised to see her picture on my home page. She had joined some social network and they had posted the announcement on all of her contacts' pages, which were accessible through hers. Two Scandinavian suitors she'd mentioned to me in early chats, "Leif Hagge" and "Hank Jacobsen" (both posing by yachts), had "friends" in the hundreds, nearly all of them middle-aged Third World cuties looking for a better future in Europe. Quite possibly Silvia was being approached by international prostitution rings—cyberpimps.

I hesitated, because I'd been working so hard to drive this whole episode out of my life—but her brazen opportunism, still shopping around after all the havoc she'd wreaked, was so grossly uncouth, and the opportunity so ripe, that I couldn't pass it up. I wrote in her "Comment" window: "Buyer beware. She's a filthy tramp, a gold-digging visa bride who will stab you in the back at the very first chance."

So shoot me. It was fun, and it took her two days to remove it, either because she didn't notice or didn't know how. I must have done *somebody* some good.

What I didn't see coming was a second wave of emptiness, at about the three-month mark, that wasn't so much about Silvia as the relationship itself, as a third person: my relationship with the relationship, or the space it took up in my life. Suddenly, after the hurt and resentment subsided and I no longer pined for treasures I couldn't get back (if I'd ever actually had them), I found myself looking at the dry bed of an ocean that was once there and now stared back at me in all its nothingness: what was my life about now? I had to find an answer.

I turned to friends and family: they were still there, and welcomed me back, as if from a long trip. I noticed the warm deference I was accorded by people at work: clerks, bailiffs, attorneys, judges, cleaning staff, cafeteria workers. I returned their morning greetings with gratitude and appreciation; the workplace I had adopted for Silvia's sake had become a second home, and the courthouse community was my community. I *did* have a life! And it was a good one. But the past still came back to bite me once in a while.

I'd finally relinquished her, but my thoughts would turn again to Silvia. How diminished, cheapened and belittled I felt, her betrayal and unfaithfulness not as hurtful as her base, wanton disregard for the moments of soaring greatness and awesome beauty we had created together. If none of that held sway with her, my presence in her life had had no meaning. If I had made her a woman, as she'd breathed into my ear one luminous night, Dirk had made her a whore, in her darkest hour.

That's what I so despised about her duplicity: blowing off not just me but her own dreams of boundless passion, a treasure she'd never get the remotest glimpse of from a bottom feeder like Dirk, a philistine, a jerk. I never expected any woman to fully share my blind faith in absolute transcendence through perfect love, indistinctly carnal and sublime. I myself could never explain it, but felt a certainty about it, an inner knowledge I longed to share with a willing partner. "It's all culture," Silvia once had said. She'd opened the door... and then slammed it shut.

Etilio had quipped earlier that when two men fight over a woman, the loser gets to keep her. He felt that Silvia's many failings made her unworthy of my efforts to reclaim her, and that the trashing she'd probably get at the end of all her manipulations would be the most fitting end to this unwholesome charade. I agreed, but still loved her, at the time, from the bottom of my heart, with irrational, gut-wrenching passion (and possibly a touch of psychosis); I'd give her the benefit of the doubt to the very end. The end, at last, had arrived: she'd finally gone too far, even for me.

Paola

My friend Roberto came from a once-powerful Nicaraguan family. In the eighties we'd been roommates in New York and I helped him adapt to American egalitarianism—petty concerns like picking up after himself and doing the dishes were completely foreign to his upbringing. He was reservedly fond of me, because he—of all people—felt that I didn't take reality seriously enough, as I made no provision for my own material comfort and long-term wherewithal. That was many years earlier, before I had children, but he still wasn't too sure about me.

Women, on the other hand, I took *too* seriously, he said. Silvia had been to his place with me once, newly arrived, and was aghast at his slovenly quarters. Yet when she had a chance to chat with him out of earshot from me, she vented freely about *my* indolence and irresponsibility. "That woman doesn't love you *at all*," he told me later, amazed at how thoroughly she berated me. After we broke up, he advised me to set up a sex fund and just get laid with call girls when the "need" arose, on a monthly basis.

"Once a month?" I retorted, appalled.

"Well, you're not getting *any* now, are you?" He had a point, so I looked into it and found a pretty escort who called herself Lorena. She was Colombian (this was going to be interesting) and very animated on the phone. As soon as she opened the door to her shabby motel room I told her that I, the paying customer, had the right to choose my own name for her, and she'd thenceforth be known as Paola (Paola was a hot Italian girl, a dancer, that got away in college, so the role-play was a comeback, of sorts).

She had the tiniest Little Black Dress— a sheath, a second skin—that came off instantly to reveal a perky, lithe anatomy that, unlike so many Colombian women, was surgically unassisted or, as she put it, "all natural." She said she was twenty-three. Feeling conversational, I informed her that it was my first time with a... well, with a *professional.*

"Right," she said, sarcastically. "And next, you're going to tell me you're a virgin."

"Well, no, actually," I rejoined, grinning. "But I was hoping maybe *you* might be."

The joke put her in a good mood.

I treated her the same way I ever treated women I had sex with, paying attention to her satisfaction, but she acted as if something wasn't right. "Do you want me to suck you now?" she asked, evidently standard procedure. "What's the hurry?" I asked. She reached for a condom from a multicolored assortment on the nightstand. I insisted: "Don't you like what we're doing?" She chuffed and dropped her shoulders, as if talking to a child: "Well, of course. I'm not made of stone. But you're a client, not my boyfriend."

"You have a *boyfriend?*" I blurted.

We lapsed into lighthearted banter, and she waxed philosophical about the world's oldest profession. "They ought to erect us a monument," she mused, resuming her duties. I suggested a giant vagina that traffic could go through in and out of some fun town like Paris or San Francisco. As she labored to bring my penis to attention, I asked her if she saw her clients' ejaculations as career achievements, and did she rate them.

"I must be one of your toughest clients," I offered, by way of consolation.

"Come om," she gluggled. "Your hour's ummost up."

"No talking with your mouth full," I answered, profoundly amused. I felt a pleasant tingle, but our fine-feathered friend refused to cooperate—no monument for Paola. "Fucking traitor," I groused, and noticed her cringing, probably alert to any early hint of psychotic behavior. "No, I mean, our friend down there," I explained, signaling groinward. "Oh," she said, releasing it. "Maybe it's time to find new friends." "What do you think I'm doing?" I cracked, grabbing her crotch, and she let out a delightful peal of wanton laughter.

"Never mind, Paola. You've done your job," I said, and began to dress.

"Really?"

I reassured her: "Yes. You've treated me very well, dear."

I still *was* a virgin, I guess, at least in that respect. I came away comparing the moral worth of a woman who openly sells her body to that of one who pretends not to, yet always expects something in return for sex, and will dump a true lover for a more advantageous option. I felt a fondness for Paola, but I'd just proven to myself that I couldn't fuck her or anyone else in that position. As I left I offered to take her out for dinner sometime, when she was "off-duty," but she never called.

I had noticed Dirk's car, the Beedl, parked a couple of blocks around the corner from the courthouse, and assumed at first he had an office there, because the townhouses on that block were mostly businesses, antique shops and the like, and something in my conversations with Silvia had given me the impression that he lived in the suburbs. On another occasion I saw the Mercedes, too, but when I saw both parked together, on the street, I realized he lived there, which I confirmed with an Internet search. He'd been right under my nose all along.

After lunch one Monday I saw the Beedl waiting at a stoplight, Dirk's face masked by windshield glare. I paused to light a cigarette, affecting poised nonchalance for his benefit. He couldn't miss me, standing at the corner as the light turned green. The next morning, as I sat smoking in a patio outside the courthouse, he drove by again, in the Drmboat, headed north. This time he couldn't see me, but I saw him clearly, hunched over the steering wheel, his back describing a forty-five-degree arc, maybe sixty—from the side, a striking view.

Two days in a row! I took it as a bad omen, a harbinger of unpleasant tidings, the foul stench of perfidy thick in the air. Why was he driving his Sunday cruiser on a Tuesday? Was it he in the Beedl the day before? The answer came Wednesday on my way to work. Again the stage was set by traffic signals: the last car turning right from the street I was about to cross was the Beedl, and the driver was Marcela. The convertible broke down, I surmised, or was repossessed, so they went running back to Dirk.

I thought I had done a good job of putting all my feelings in order, yet I snapped. And I was angry that I snapped. I was even angry that I was angry; why should I care at all? Yielding to a reckless impulse, I wrote a windshield note for Dirk, picking up on the same theme as the last one—but a stronger dose, because he *still* didn't get it: he was supposed to be out of the picture. The final deal breaker with Silvia had been her crass insensitivity, but I wanted to have something I could still respect her for; that was gone with this new proof of her venal concupiscence. So I wrote:

"Last fuck: March 11, 2011. I'm afraid you'll still have to wait almost nine more months for Silvia's final divorce." Not bad, for openers. I wanted to sow unease, to cast the impression that I could have her anytime, thus compromising future stolen intimacy. "Until then, she's still committing adultery. Virginia code 18.2-366: check it out. Unless maybe anal doesn't count. Oh, but that's illegal in Virginia, too... should've kept my mouth shut! You won't rat me out, will you, bro?"

Bad logic, but I wasn't too worried about that; he'd never catch the fallacy.

"Quite possibly immigration fraud, too," I continued. "But I think Homeland Security has overblown the whole illegal alien thing, especially that part about crimes against morals and decency, the surest way to trigger deportation proceedings—just a phone call away. Really, though, screwing around behind your husband's back doesn't mean you're going to blow up the World Trade Center, right? And God knows there's no shortage of moral turpitude right here in America. Plus we can always use a few more Latina hotties to spice up the meat market."

I couldn't believe I was doing this. But I also couldn't stop: "Maybe by March you'll figure out who the real swine is. Meantime, enjoy! Why let a perfectly good visa go to waste? I also spent a couple grand on plastic surgery, so she's good to go. She wants a boob job, too, but I don't think she needs one—maybe later. You might have to shell out for the kids' college, though. I paid for their last three semesters in Colombia while they were waiting to get here. Too bad their mom dumped me right after they arrived. I guess that's where *you* come in, Johnny-on-the-spot."

I took a jab at his two-timing on the Filipina lady—though by then he'd probably already dumped her.

"Have you told your girlfriend yet? It's the honorable thing to do, you know, even if she is 'old and ugly,' as Silvia puts it. I can see you wanting to upgrade to a lower-mileage exotic if you don't get the same rise from the old one anymore. But the betrayal of trust, of years of loyal commitment, can be excruciatingly painful. A good woman doesn't deserve that. Being the righteous dude that you are, I'm sure I don't need to spell it out for you.

"Good talking to you, bro. Silvia's *your* bitch now. The love thing finally got old —I'm done with that scheming, deceitful reptile. The rage is harder to deal with, but knowing that I've brought true love and happiness to a decent, respectable man makes me feel much better. Thanks, and may you reap the full benefits of your new acquisition. Until she lands a better deal, that is. Ask her about Leif Hagge, or Hank Jacobsen, among other current prospects."

I'd reached the pinnacle of sincerity, so I signed off sweetly, "The Swine."

It was lunchtime and I strolled over by Dirk's to drop off the note, but neither car was there. I returned after work and the Mercedes was parked out front. After the first note he had told Silvia (when she was seeing both of us) that if I didn't stop bothering him he'd have to stop using the Beedl, assuming that I didn't know the other car. Now he'd know that I did, so maybe he'd have to buy a new one. For a scary security hack, he was rather a wuss. When the deed was done I drove away, wickedly pleased with myself, the perfect bastard.

Driving aimlessly around after an early dinner (because I'd skipped lunch), instead of going home I found myself wandering in the direction of Claudio's, a DC salsa club where my friend Ernie Valera's group sometimes played. There was a sense of freedom about me; I wanted to step out for the evening. Halfway there, the phone rang.

"Daniel, this is Dirk Brown."

"Hey, Dirk, how are you doing?" I answered with earnest cheer.

"You better stop putting notes on my car," he said, leaving out the auxiliary (again), "or I'm going to do something about it."

Brown... Dirk Brown: what a fine name for a rat, I mused, elated at the confirmation that my nasty message had drawn blood.

"Don't mention it, Dirk; glad to help."

He threatened me further: "I'm going to report you to your superiors, tell them what you've been up to." Oh, pooh, I thought. He might as well go tell my mother. Better yet, his mother could tell my mother, and the old girls could settle the boys' little squabble. "Do what you have to do, bro. You're a big boy now. I'm sure you can tell right from wrong."

Repetitively, he droned on: "I have the notes and I'll show them to your boss if you bother me again." For the life of me I couldn't figure out why he'd want to share such tawdry information about himself and Silvia with a Supreme Court division chief. But I feigned alarm: "Gosh, Dirk, that could ruin my career." He persisted: "Well, that's what I'll do next time you put a note on my car." This was getting tiresome. "Dirk," I said, "it strikes me that you're being a bit ungrateful. After everything I've done for you, this is how you pay me, with threats?"

But he'd already hung up. I parsed the conversation: his listless tone, the impotent threat, mechanically repeated. And then it hit me: it wasn't his idea! I could just see Silvia next to him, prodding him to be a man, to get even with me, to *do something* about it. Such lackluster performance: whatever happened to knocking my head off? I shouldn't have been so hard on him; as we say about Texas, he'd stolen her fair and square. Feeling a rush of compassion, I texted to the number he'd just supplied me: "You're good, Dirk. I'm done. Thank me later."

Mock Turtle Soup

Ahh, Dirk—what a guy! During our first barroom conversation (not the one when he threatened to kill me) I drew him into talking about family, always a good way to gain insight into someone's character and value system. He mentioned a daughter, whom he described, in typical breeder's lingo, as "well turned out." She was black—not, as I first thought, because he'd been married to a black woman, but because, as Silvia told me later, Tiffany was adopted.

She was about the same age as Verónica, Dirk's "princess." He told me that she lived in Charlottesville, where Lizzie went to school. I saw her in a modeling website, displaying her talent in a black-and-white nude shot —tastefully draped, however, in a colorized American flag, delicately arranged to cover her intimate parts. She was more of a mulatta—a rather homely one, at that, but shapely and well toned: a fitting reward for some war-weary conquering hero, returning to the homeland after a tour of duty in distant Arabian deserts.

Understanding what Dirk meant by "well turned out," I realized that my earlier unease over his enthusiasm for Verónica had not been misplaced. The immodest jingoism of Tiffany's racy portfolio entry (the rest of them, forgettable yawners) illustrated with unintended poignancy that queer blend of licentious self-righteousness that defines a distinctly *gringo* ideological construct, that condones any excess so long as minimally credible argument can be made for it on grounds of national security, interest, or plain old American exceptionalism.

Hadn't Great American Poet Walt Whitman, after all, included the white beaches of Cuba among the bounteous riches bestowed by a godless universe upon our great land, along with the golden fields of windblown wheat and the purple majesty of the high sierra over which he waxed prosaic, occasionally pausing to drool over "my brood of grown and part-grown boys, who love to be with no one else so well as they love to be with me, by day to work with me, and by night to sleep with me"?[*] We've come a long way, but pederasty is still illegal.

Like Lewis Carroll's mock turtle soup, the snake oil sold by this self-published purveyor of mock grandiosity had the genuine flavor of something that didn't exist but by literal extrapolation from a predicate upon an assumption upon a conceit. It was beyond me how later scholarship mated Whitman to the towering splendor of Abraham Lincoln, a man of stark verbal elegance whose brilliant "Spot Resolutions" in Congress laid bare the sophistry with which Polk's henchmen concocted a "provocation" to justify the war on Mexico, à la Gulf of Tonkin.

---

[*] Whitman, "A Song of Joys," *Leaves of Grass*.

Silvia, like Alice in Wonderland—but, unlike Alice, blind to the absurdity of her surroundings—had scurried down the rabbit hole of the very American Dream that she professed to disdain, but repeated as farce, a caricature of the real America she would never know. The mock respectability she attained by "hooking up" with a federal rogue—despite twenty years of contrary experience, during which another rogue had defiled their marriage at every turn—was painted with the same brush as the flag that barely covered Tiffany's naked body.

Freedom

I had never really appreciated what fun it was to be a bastard, and wondered why other people did it. Now I was a member of the club. I walked jauntily into Claudio's and danced with a luscious, tall Congolese woman named Adèle, who beamed a radiant, natural joy and suffered graciously my broken French. Then I spotted another dark-skinned beauty who couldn't stop dancing, even at the bar. Her moves told me she was Colombian, probably from Buenaventura; but before I had a chance to dance with her, she was gone.

The following morning, around ten, I got a call from officer Smiley of the Leesburg police. "Mr. Durán," he started cautiously, "a Ms. Silvia Cordero came by the station to complain that you left a note on her boyfriend's car." Boyfriend... it was official, then. "Do you know her?"

"Yes, I know her. She's my lying, cheating wife."

"What about the note, Mr. Durán, did you leave that?"

"Yes. I wanted to give the bastard a piece of my mind about their affair, and maybe break them up, too, because she's also playing him. The bitch goes back and forth."

He advised me that I could be breaking the law by coming onto someone's property to leave a note on their car. But the car was on the street, I replied, and if pizza parlors can put fliers on people's windshields, so could I; the owner was free to read it or toss it.

"We just want to make sure the situation doesn't escalate, Mr. Durán," he explained. I assured him it wouldn't go an inch further. I had said my piece, and whatever the scumbag and his strumpet chose to do thereafter was no longer any business of mine. The officer thanked me and we parted cordially.

But I cheated. As soon as I hung up I texted Silvia, the first time I had addressed her in four months: "Thanks. Now the Leesburg police know all about you." I just wanted her to feel stupid. It was unfathomable what relief she imagined she would get by embarrassing herself and agent Dirk like that. Officer Smiley had read the note and told me that he found nothing threatening or illegal about it, so the only effect of bringing it to their attention was to provide the Police Department a juicy bit of gossip for the day. They probably knew Dirk, too.

I felt a strange calm. I examined the sequence of events and concluded that Silvia was still seething from the lurid details in the note, and wasn't appeased by her boyfriend's tepid drivel from the night before. I could imagine the girls, particularly Verónica, urging her to seek redress, probably driving her to the station themselves, for most likely she still had no license. I had ruined four people's days, but suddenly mine was looking a lot better. In the midst of it all, one thing was certain: this time I definitely didn't want her back.

I began to assemble a new reality, born of this corrected perspective. Things that had been hazy and confused began to fit into plausible scenarios. One of those was that the reason Silvia was so hard to get a hold of during her last trip to Colombia was that she remained in touch with Dirk all along and was putting him forward to family and friends as her new "official" benefactor. He'd probably given her money for her airfare—and for the girls', but they'd spent that part on gifts to show how well they were doing in the Promised Land. To be overheard still talking to me would stir the inbred skepticism of the *rolo* audience she sought to impress with her fairy-tale success with a new (if old) Prince Charming.

I caught on to the sleight-of-cunt Silvia pulled on me in Atlantic City, a succubus swap whereby she outdid my incubus act in Cancún. If she couldn't tell she'd been fucked in her sleep, I told her then, she also couldn't know by whom. She did precisely that to me, and I wasn't even asleep; her perverse reverse cheating was an unbelievably twisted way of getting even—and perhaps, for the moment, remaining "faithful" to Dirk. Again, I'd been a means to an end: Ashley's defloration. The stunt was wickedly brilliant, if heartless, and dangerous in every way. The Bolivian lady didn't misunderstand her daughter at all; if anything, she underestimated her... and Silvia. I'd been had, in different ways, by both.

Another realization brought about by this perceptive realignment was that even if I couldn't elucidate the myriad perplexing enigmas littering my path through life with Silvia—the unanswered inconsistencies, the lies that were clearly so even if there appeared to be no reason for them—it didn't matter, because the door had finally shut on the past, and I was on the other side. There was nothing she could say or do to hurt me, and any grotesque opinion that she or her daughters could have of me was their problem, not mine. I was free, no longer waiting for anything—or rather, for nothing.

I shared the most recent anecdote with a number of friends, who nearly unanimously rebuked my actions as childish and immature. I had always felt, though, that "maturity" is highly overrated, as "the kingdom of heaven belongs to such as these children," according to Jesus himself, on the authority of his Dad. As to the note, however, a few remarked that they enjoyed the caustic humor, though it might be more appropriate to a work of fiction than to the interaction with real life characters who could exact retribution for such brass.

The following week I returned to Claudio's. I ran into Ernie, but the band wasn't playing. Adèle wasn't there, nor the girl from Buenaventura. I danced with a Scottish girl named Roisin (pronounced *Rosheen*), trim and athletic, but I couldn't keep up with her. We took a break and leaned against a high counter, watching the other dancers. She was twenty-one and talkative, but her English was as hard to follow as her salsa, so I excused myself and extended my hand to shake hers. It was limp, which I disliked, feeling that a firm handshake bespeaks character also in a woman.

As I drove home I turned the week's events over yet again in my mind. The road ahead seemed to symbolize, rolling toward me, the promise of a better future, of events to come and make me a better man than ever before. I was tired but relieved, wounded but not beat. I had turned a new page, and I was going to make it. I remembered Rick's parting words to Ilsa in that ambiguous scene in *Casablanca*, when she may or may not have cheated on Laszlo: "We'll always have Paris." I forgave Silvia. She owes me nothing. I still have Guantánamo.

"It's all culture."

Silvia Cordero